Table of Contents

This book belongs to:

Kindergaten Skills Checklist

Language and Communication Skills

Verbal Communication: Your child should be able to communicate their thoughts and ideas in clear sentences. Encourage conversations and storytelling to build their confidence.
Examples: Saying "I want some juice", "My teddy bear is brown", or "I like playing with blocks"

Listening and Comprehension: They should follow multi-step directions. Practice this through games, such as "Please fetch the blue ball and then place it in the toy box."
Examples: "Put your toys in the box", "Please wash your hands", or "Can you find your blue shirt?"

Expanding Vocabulary: Reading together regularly can help your child learn new words and understand their meanings.

Social and Emotional Skills

Interacting with Peers: Your child should be learning to share, take turns, and cooperate with others. Regular playdates can provide valuable opportunities to practice these skills.
Examples: Sharing a toy during playtime, waiting their turn on the swing, or playing a simple board game with family.

Expressing and Understanding Emotions: They should be able to name their feelings and show empathy towards others. Use storybooks to discuss different emotions and how to handle them.
Examples: Saying "I'm upset because...", recognizing a crying friend may be sad, or comforting a sibling who's fallen

Demonstrating Independence: Your child should be able to accomplish simple tasks independently, such as getting dressed or packing their backpack. Praise them for these achievements to promote self-confidence.

Kindergaten Skills Checklist

Cognitive Skills and Mathematics

Understanding Numbers: Your child should recognize and write numbers up to 10, and count up to 20 or beyond. Counting everyday items, like steps or pieces of fruit, can reinforce this skill.
Examples: Counting up to 20, recognizing the number "5" on a sign, or counting how many fingers they have.

Simple Arithmetic: Introduce your child to basic addition and subtraction using visual aids, like apples or building blocks. If you start with five blocks and take two away, how many are left?

Recognizing Patterns: They should be able to identify simple patterns and sequences. Use coloured blocks or beads to demonstrate and create patterns together.
Examples: Sorting blocks by colour or recognizing a pattern on their clothes

Understanding Shapes and Sizes: Your child should identify common shapes and understand concepts of size such as bigger, smaller, taller, shorter. Shape and size sorting toys can be excellent tools for this.

Physical Development Skills

Gross Motor Skills: Your child should demonstrate abilities such as hopping, skipping, and throwing a ball. Provide plenty of opportunities for outdoor play.
Examples: Jumping with both feet or climbing playground equipment

Fine Motor Skills: They should be able to hold and use a pencil, cut with safety scissors, and do up buttons. Activities like drawing, colouring, and crafting can aid in developing these skills.
Examples: Drawing shapes, using scissors to cut along a line, or buttoning their own shirt

Remember, every child develops at their own pace and it's okay if your child hasn't mastered all these skills yet. What's most important is to keep engaging them in activities that help them learn and grow while making sure they enjoy the process.

Look at Me!

Look into a mirror. Now, draw a picture of yourself. Print your name.

Colour Review

Colour Review

Read the colour word in each crayon. Colour each crayon the correct colour.

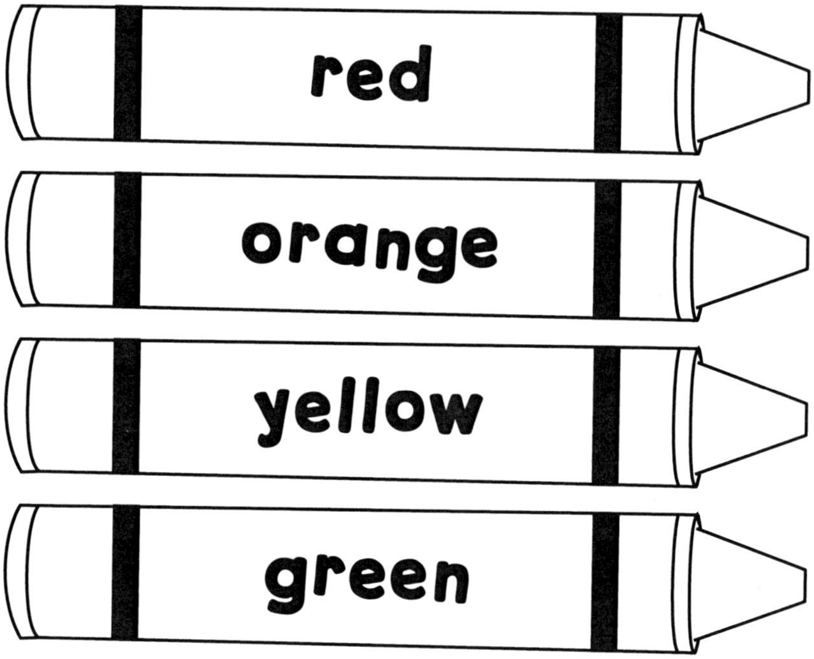

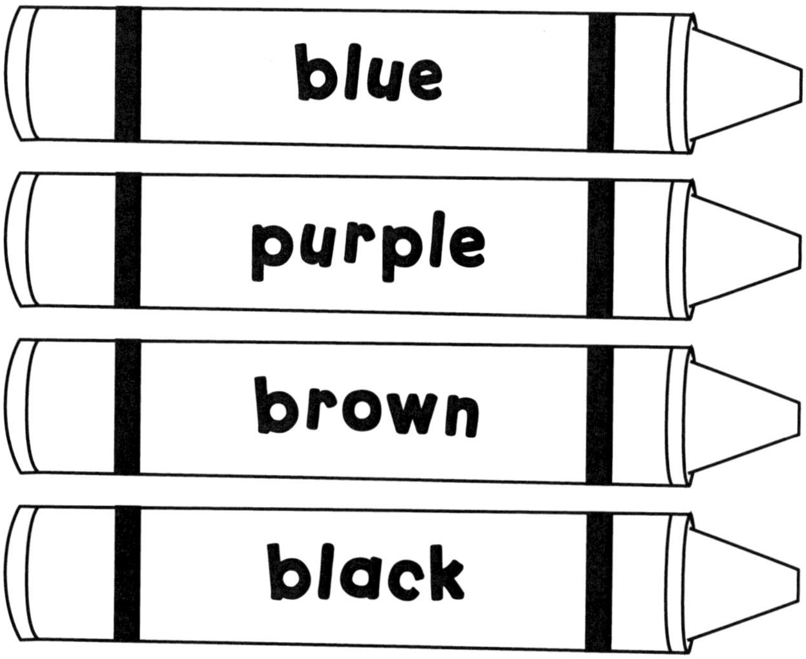

Rainbow Fun

Colour the rainbow.

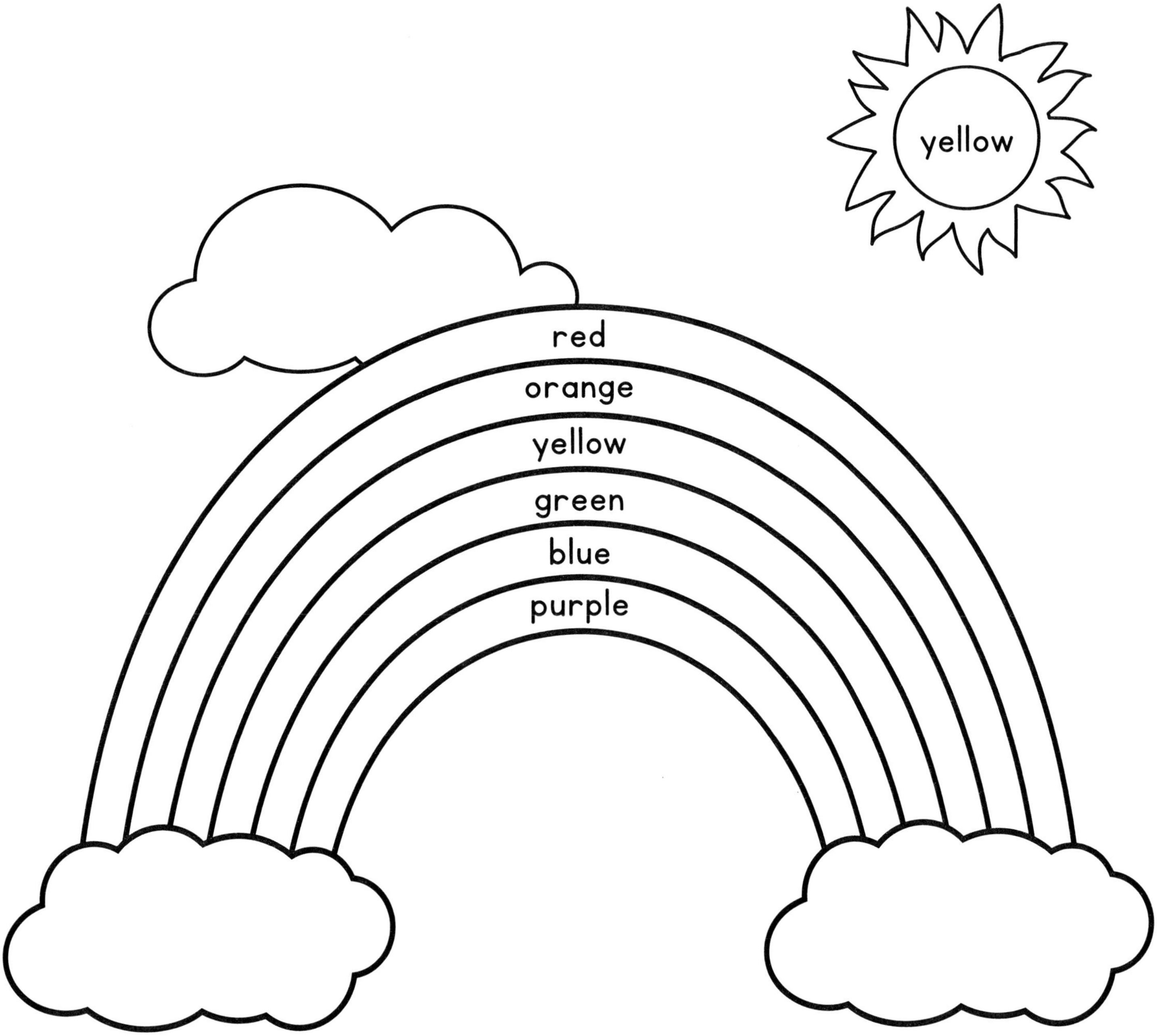

Colour Match Up

Match the crayon to the correct object.
Colour the crayons and the objects.

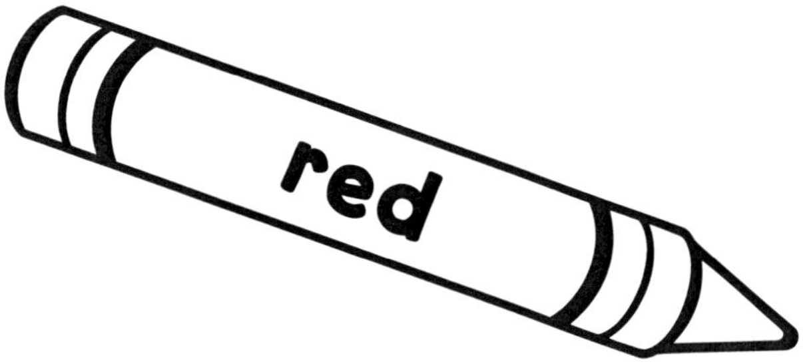

apple

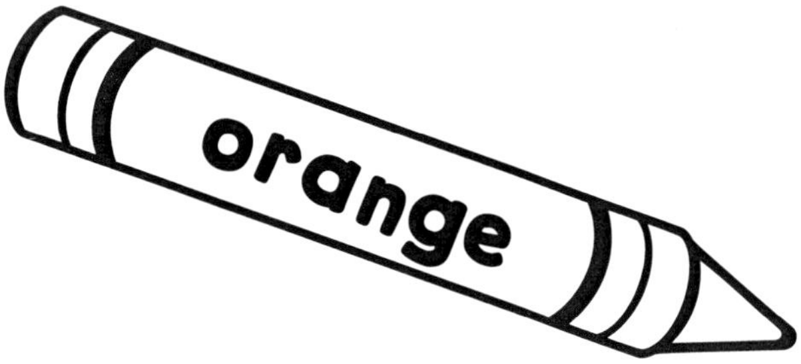

banana

leaf

orange

Colour Match Up

Match the crayon to the correct object.

Colour the crayons and the objects.

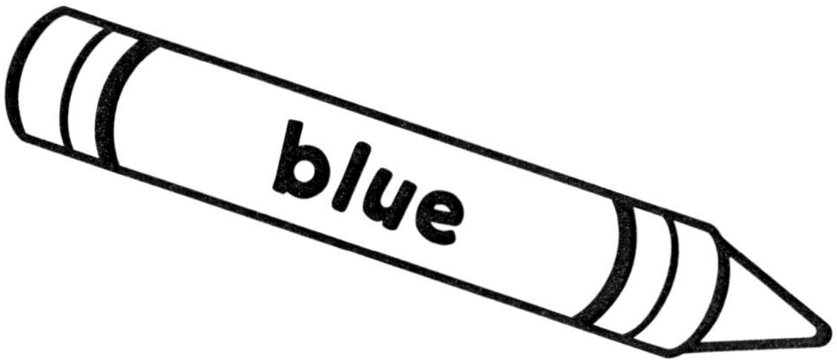

acorn

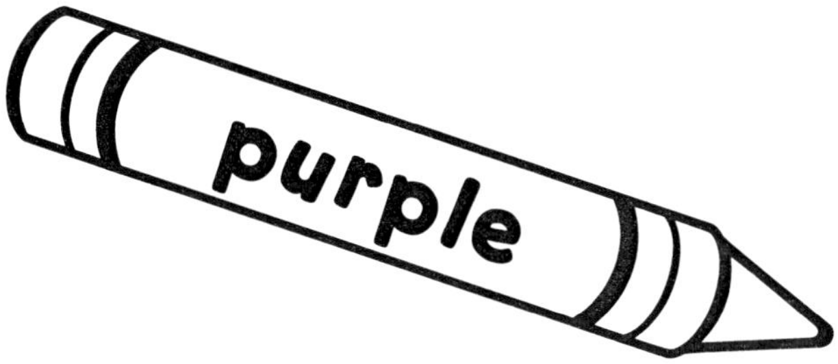

jeans

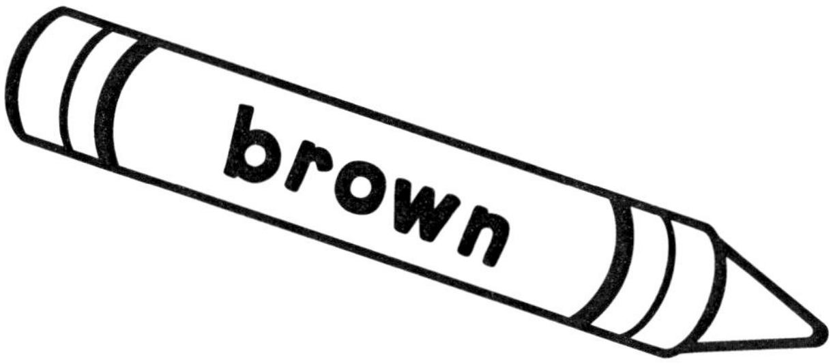

kettle

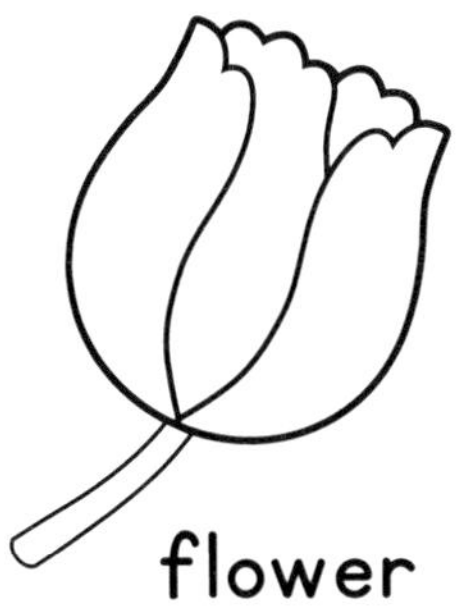

flower

Colouring Fun

Colour the gumballs in the machine.

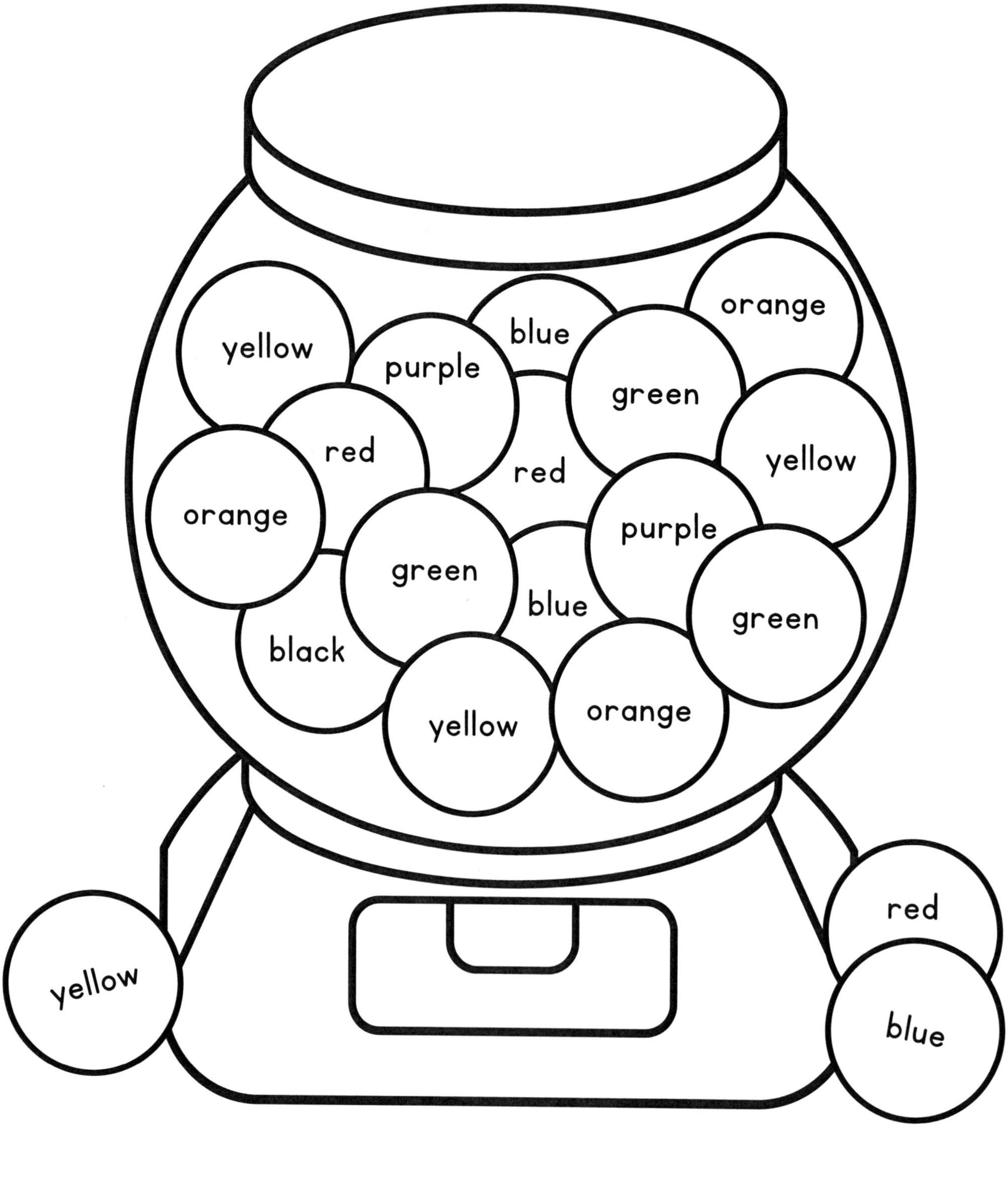

Printing and Alphabet Skills

Letter A is for Apple

Colour the capital A's. red

Colour the lowercase a's. blue

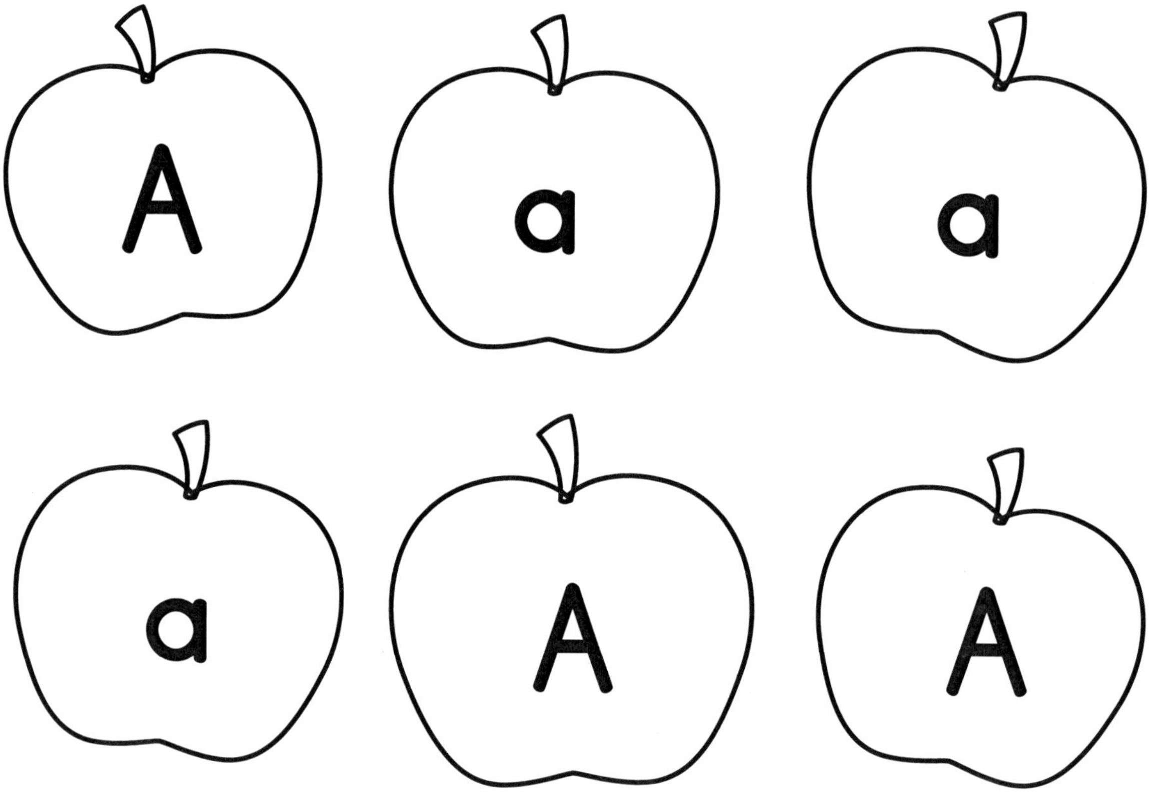

Trace and print the letters on each line.

Circle your best letter on each line.

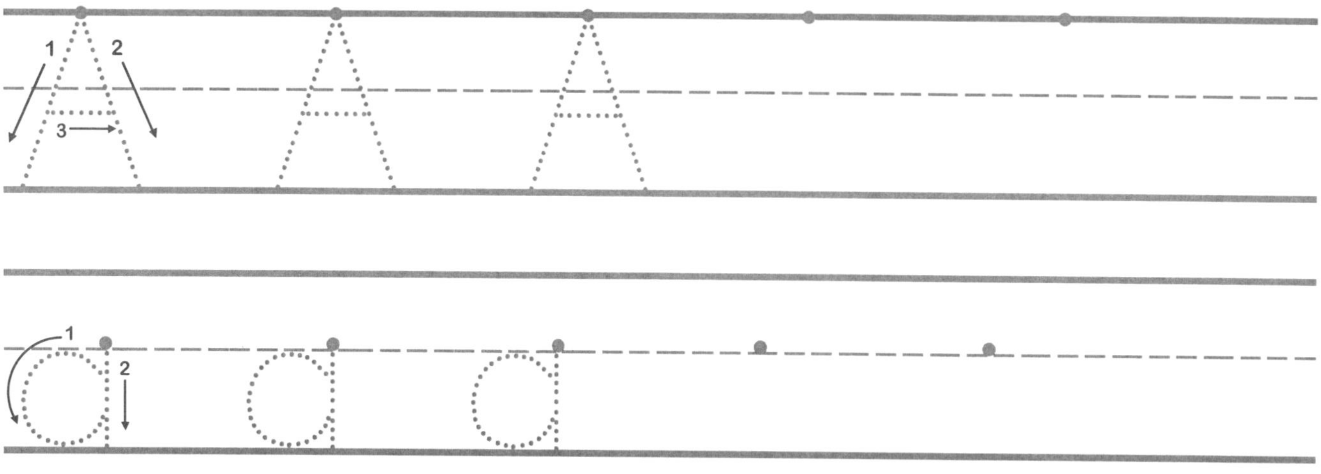

Letter A Practice

Say the name of each object aloud.
Connect "A" to every object that begins with the letter "A."

A

Trace and print the letters on each line.
Circle your best letter on each line.

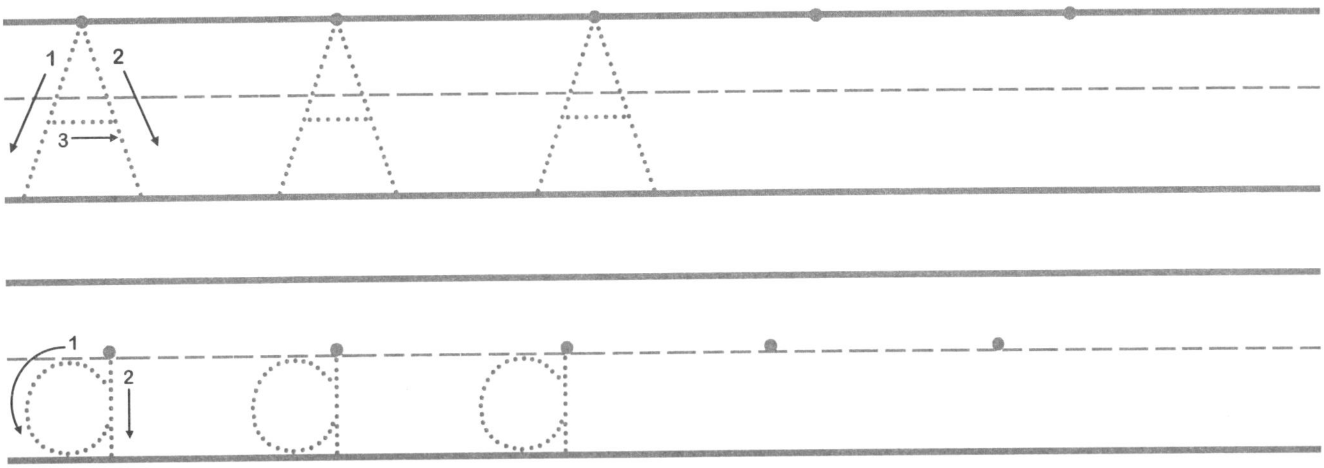

Letter B is for Berry

Colour the capital B's. blue

Colour the lowercase b's. purple

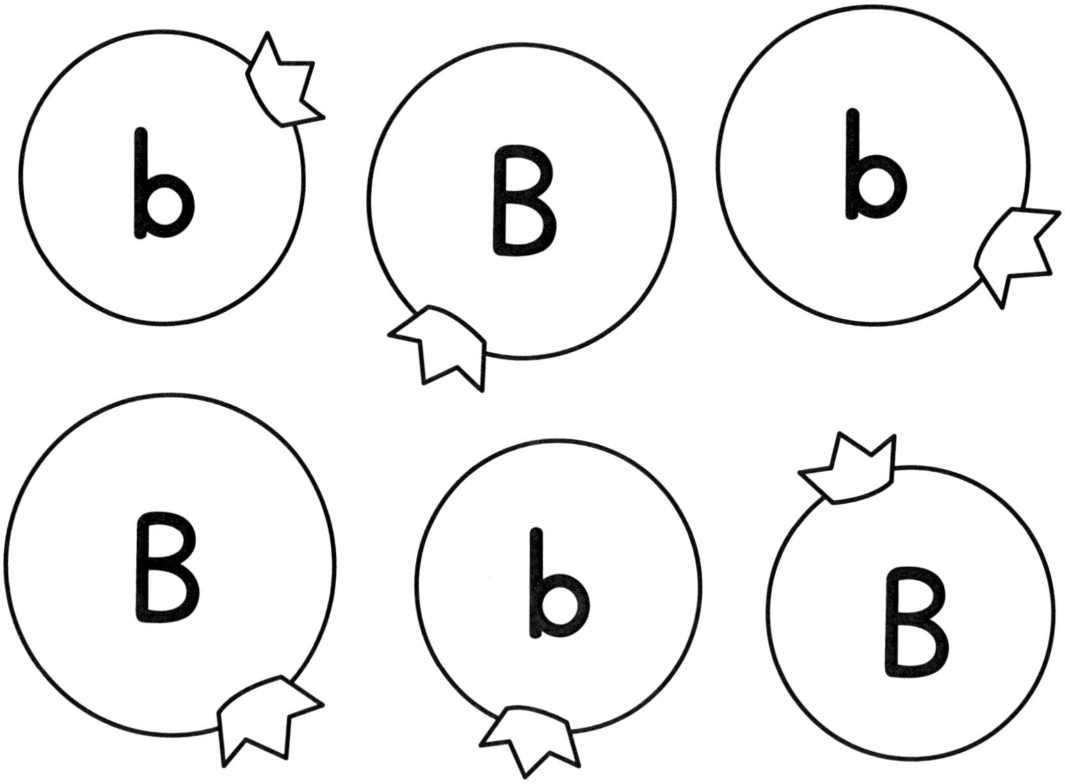

Trace and print the letters on each line.

Circle your best letter on each line.

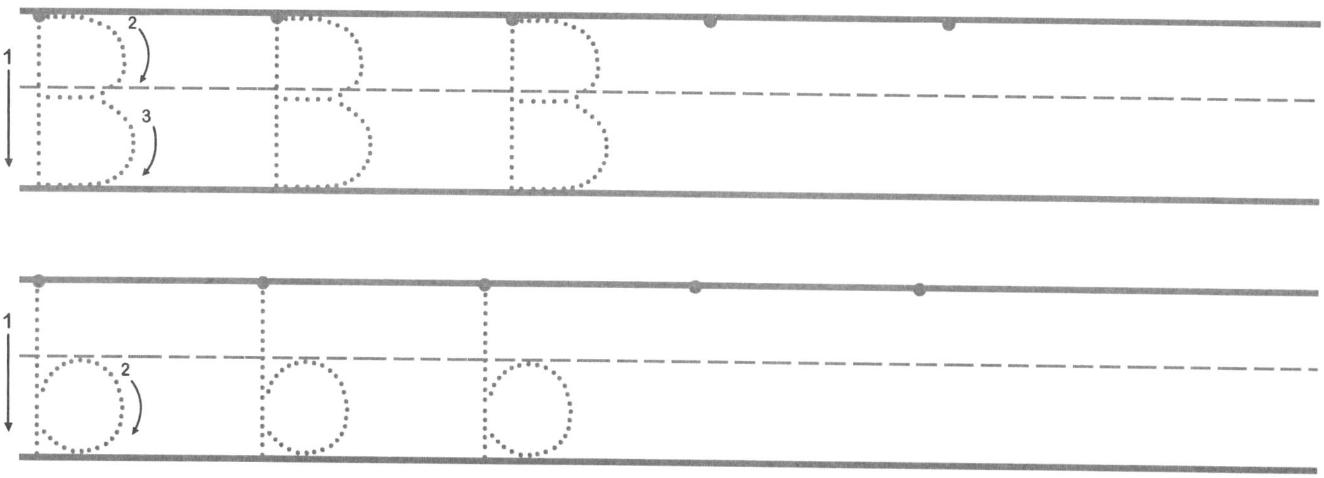

Letter B Practice

Say the name of each object aloud.
Connect "B" to every object that begins with the letter "B."

B

Trace and print the letters on each line.
Circle your best letter on each line.

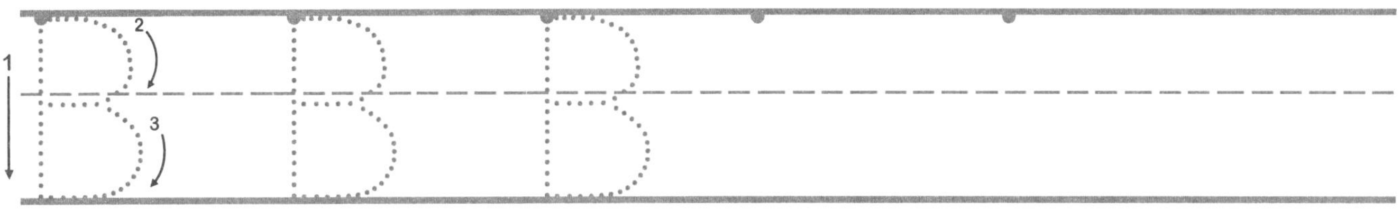

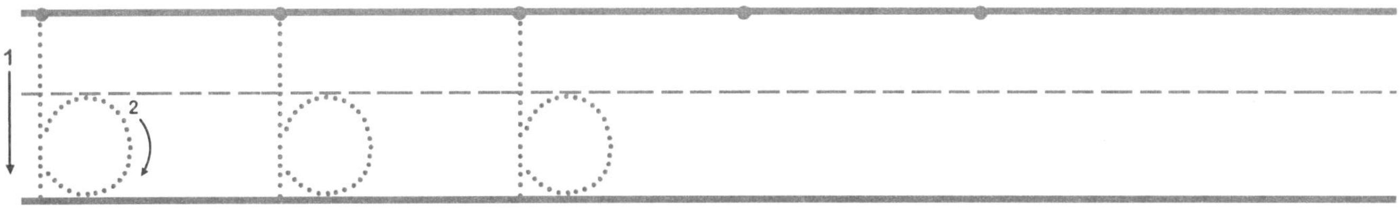

Letter C is for Cup

Colour the capital C's. green

Colour the lowercase c's. yellow

Trace and print the letters on each line.
Circle your best letter on each line.

Letter C Practice

Say the name of each object aloud.
Connect "C" to every object that begins with the letter "C."

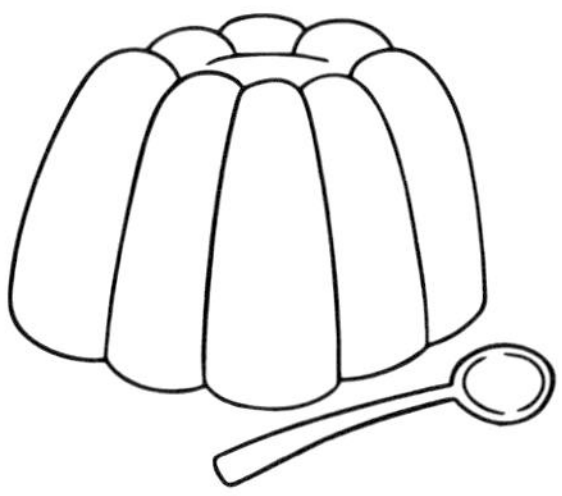

C

Trace and print the letters on each line.
Circle your best letter on each line.

1 C C C

1 c c c

Letter D is for Dish

Colour the capital D's. orange
Colour the lowercase d's. red

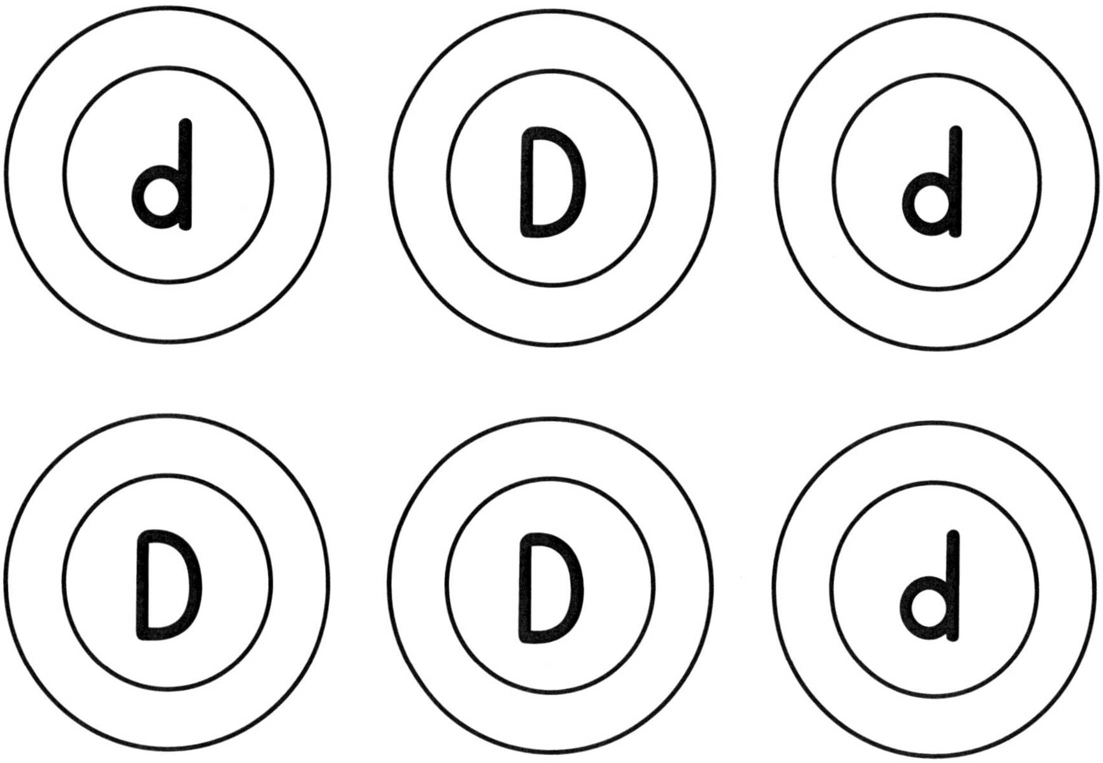

Trace and print the letters on each line.
Circle your best letter on each line.

D D D

d d d

Letter D Practice

Say the name of each object aloud.
Connect "D" to every object that begins with the letter "D."

D

Trace and print the letters on each line.
Circle your best letter on each line.

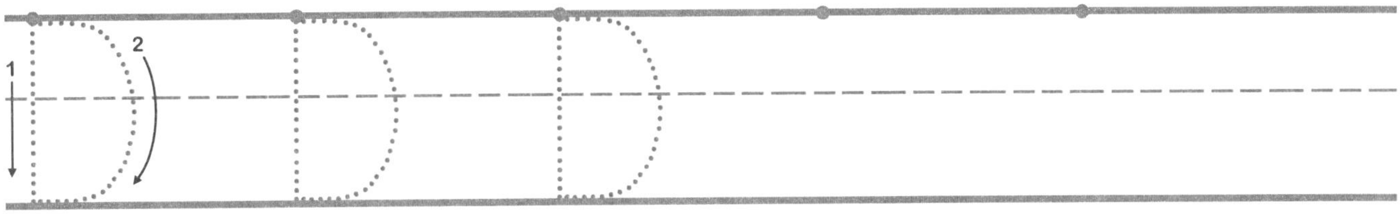

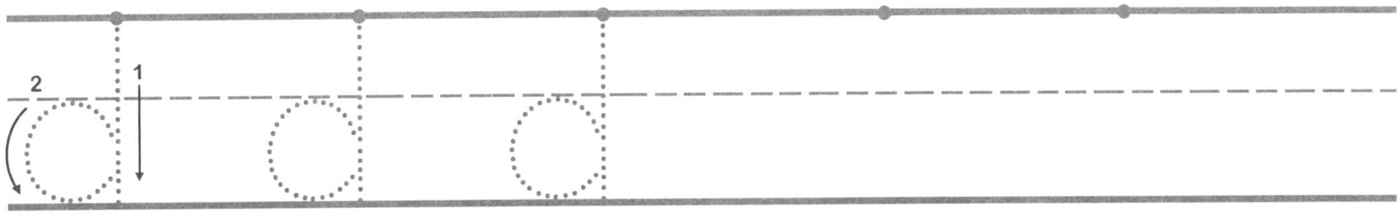

Letter E is for Egg

Colour the capital E's. blue
Colour the lowercase e's. green

E E e

e E e

Trace and print the letters on each line.
Circle your best letter on each line.

Letter E Practice

Say the name of each object aloud.
Connect "E" to every object that begins with the letter "E."

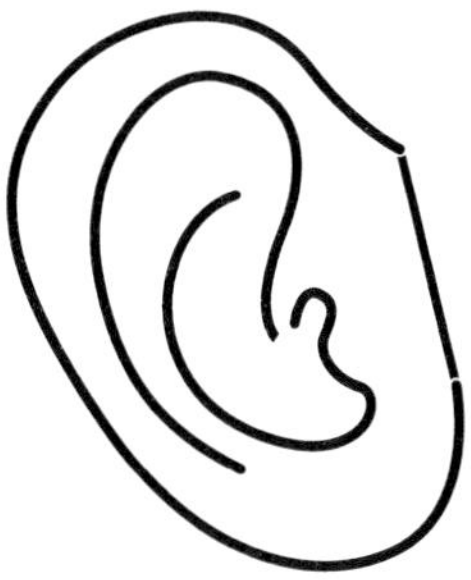

E

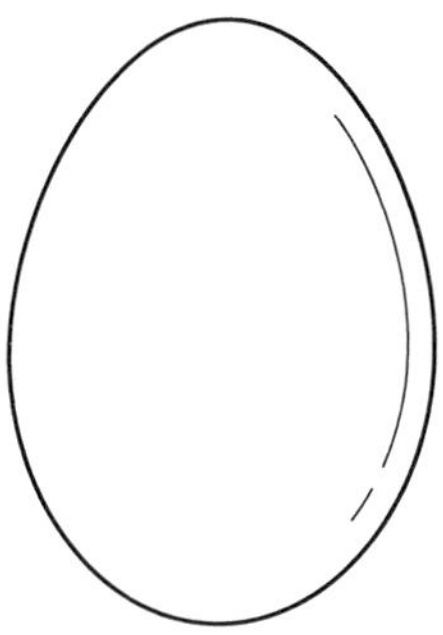

Trace and print the letters on each line.
Circle your best letter on each line.

Letter F is for Flag

Colour the capital F's. yellow
Colour the lowercase f's. purple

Trace and print the letters on each line.
Circle your best letter on each line.

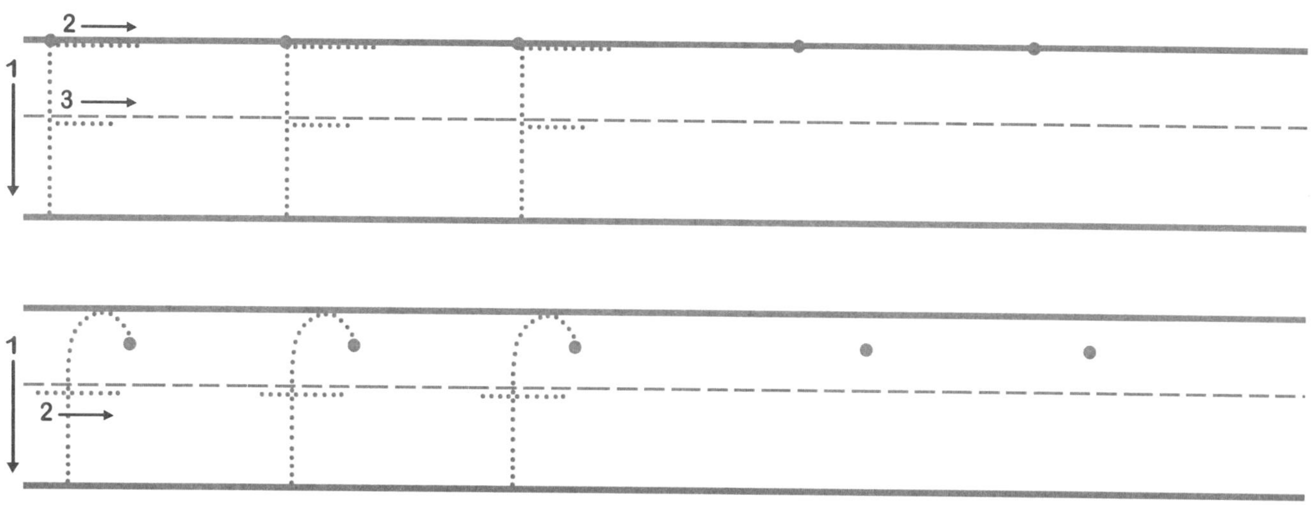

Letter F Practice

Say the name of each object aloud.
Connect "F" to every object that begins with the letter "F."

F

Trace and print the letters on each line.
Circle your best letter on each line.

Letter G is for Gift

Colour the capital G's. red

Colour the lowercase g's. orange

Trace and print the letters on each line.

Circle your best letter on each line.

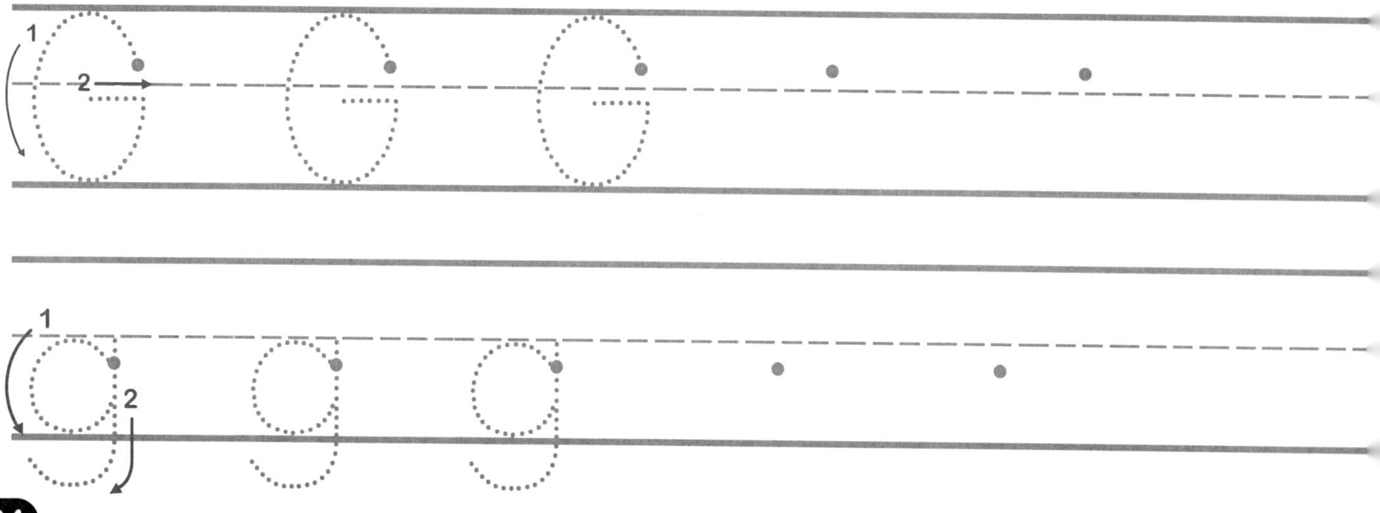

Letter G Practice

Say the name of each object aloud.
Connect "G" to every object that begins with the letter "G."

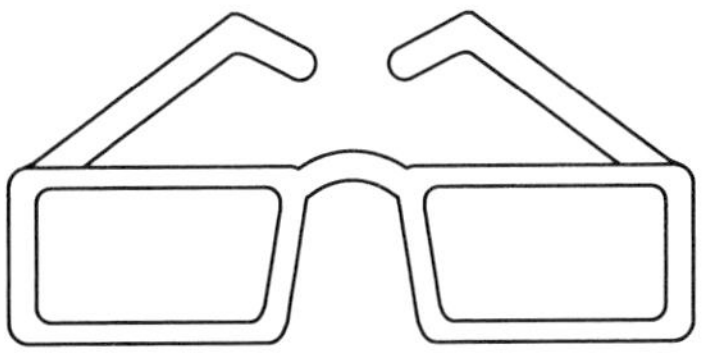

G

Trace and print the letters on each line.
Circle your best letter on each line.

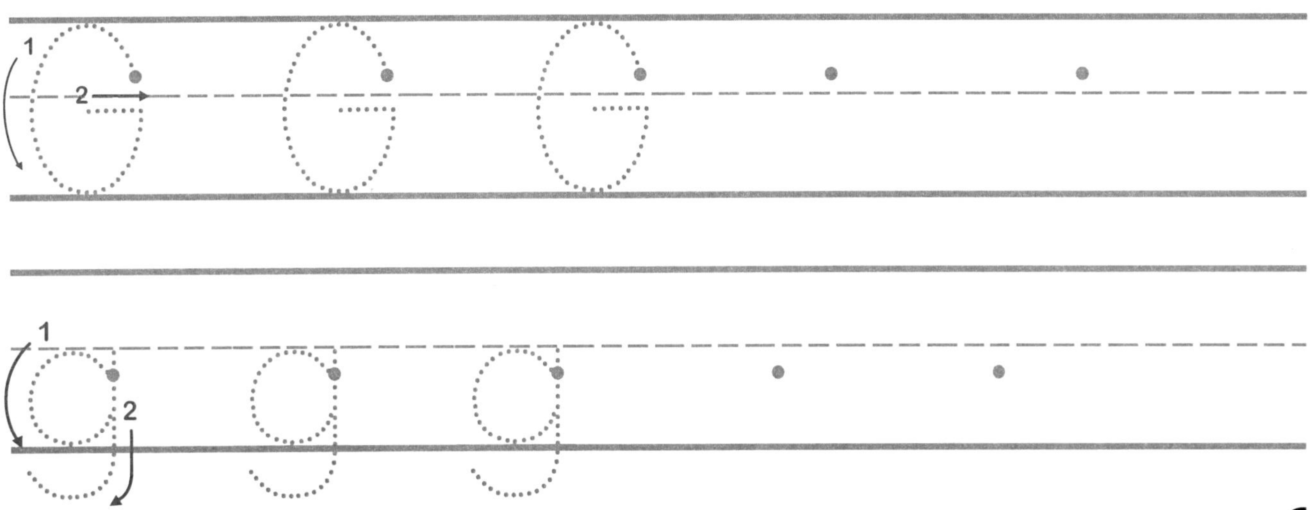

Letter H is for Hat

Colour the capital H's. blue
Colour the lowercase h's. purple

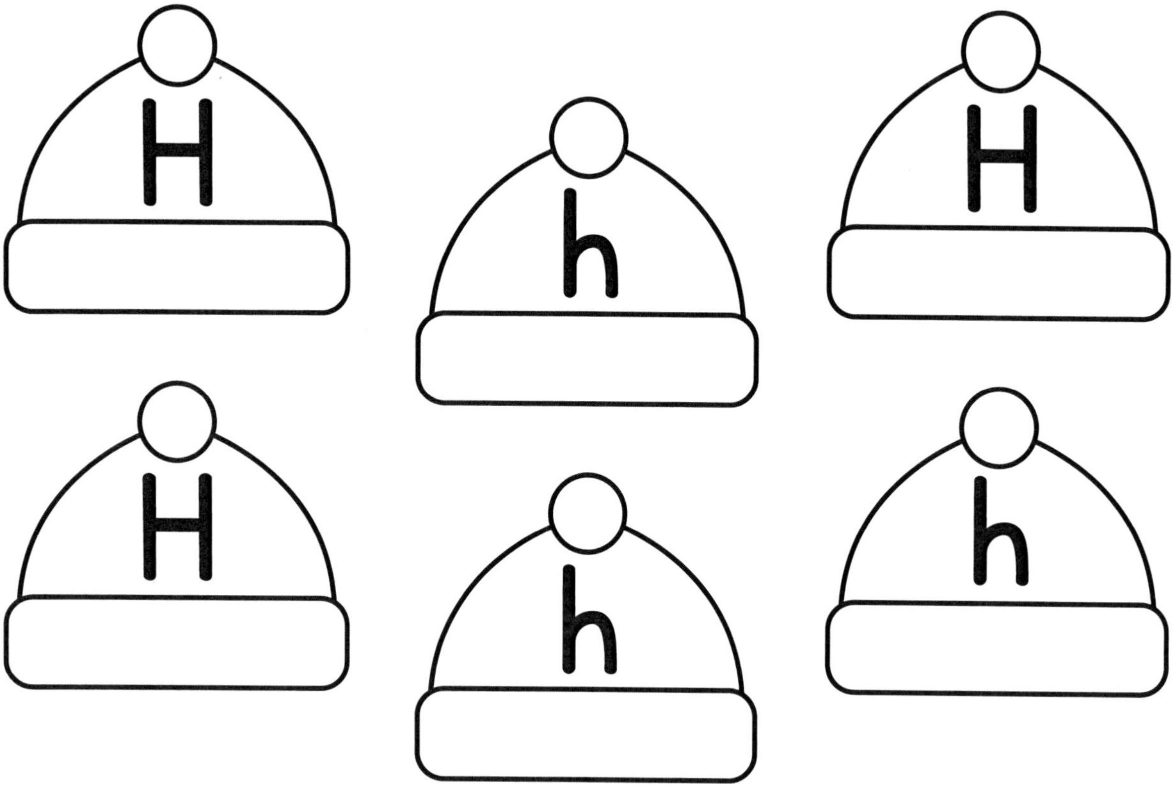

Trace and print the letters on each line.
Circle your best letter on each line.

1 2 3

1 2

Letter H Practice

Say the name of each object aloud.
Connect "H" to every object that begins with the letter "H."

H

Trace and print the letters on each line.
Circle your best letter on each line.

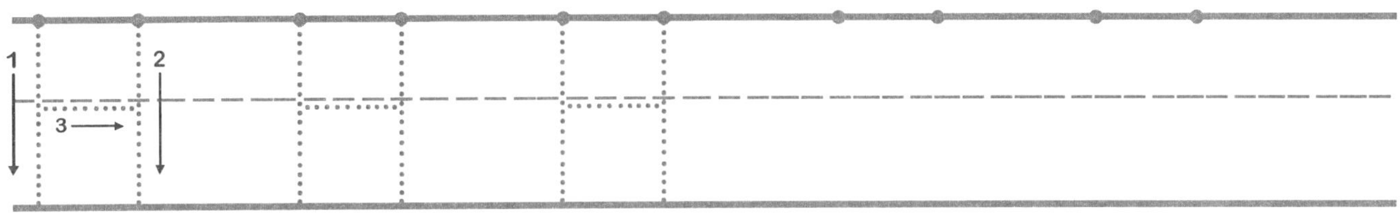

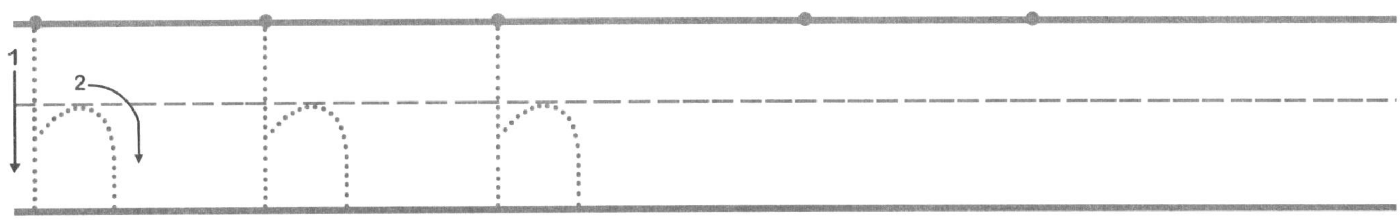

Letter I is for Insect

Colour the capital I's. 

Colour the lowercase i's. 

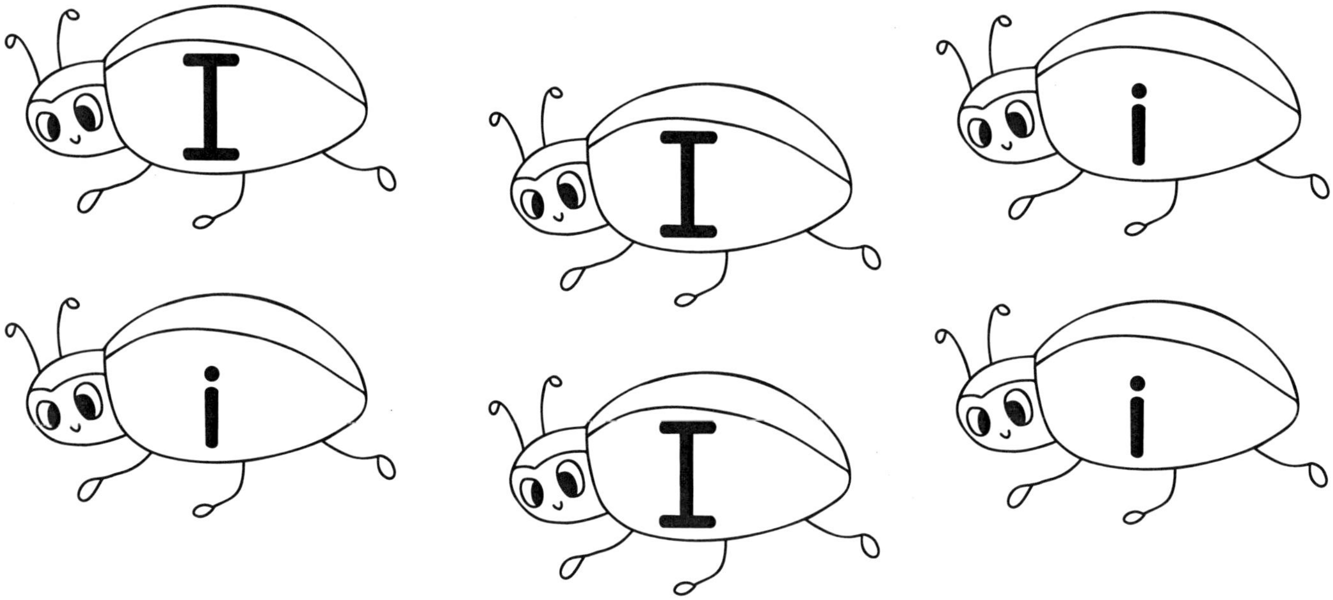

Trace and print the letters on each line.
Circle your best letter on each line.

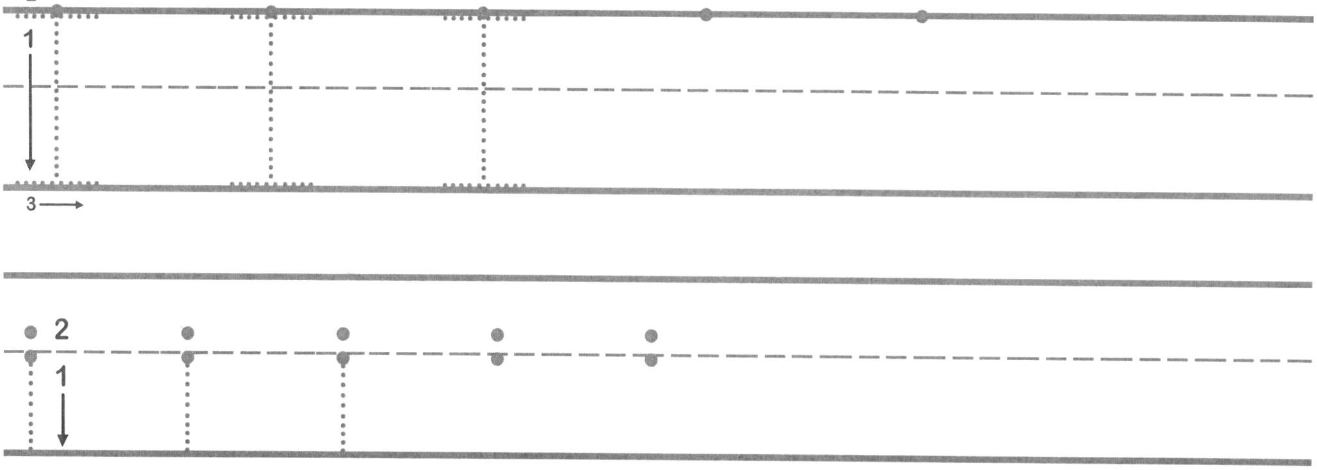

Letter I Practice

Say the name of each object aloud.
Connect "I" to every object that begins with the letter "I."

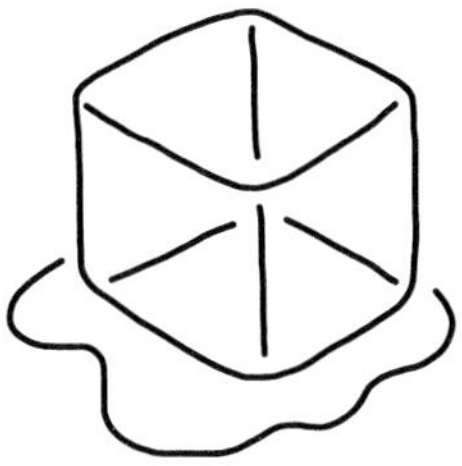

I

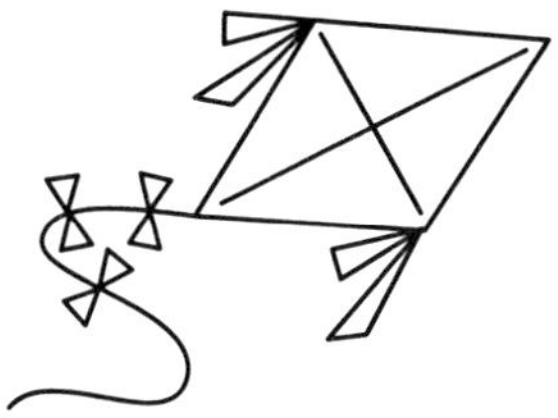

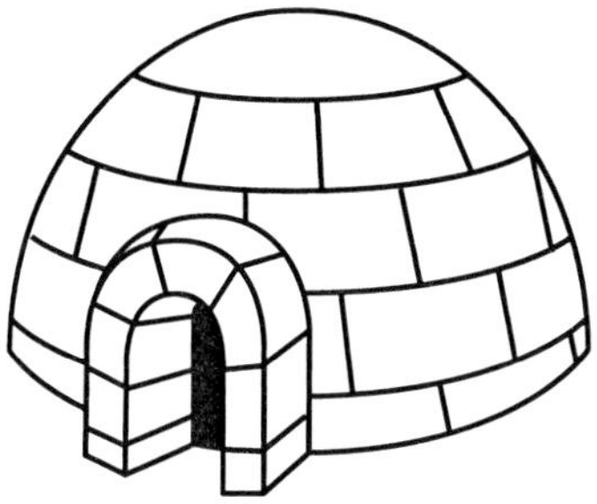

Trace and print the letters on each line.
Circle your best letter on each line.

Letter J is for Jam

Colour the capital J's. red

Colour the lowercase j's. orange

Trace and print the letters on each line.

Circle your best letter on each line.

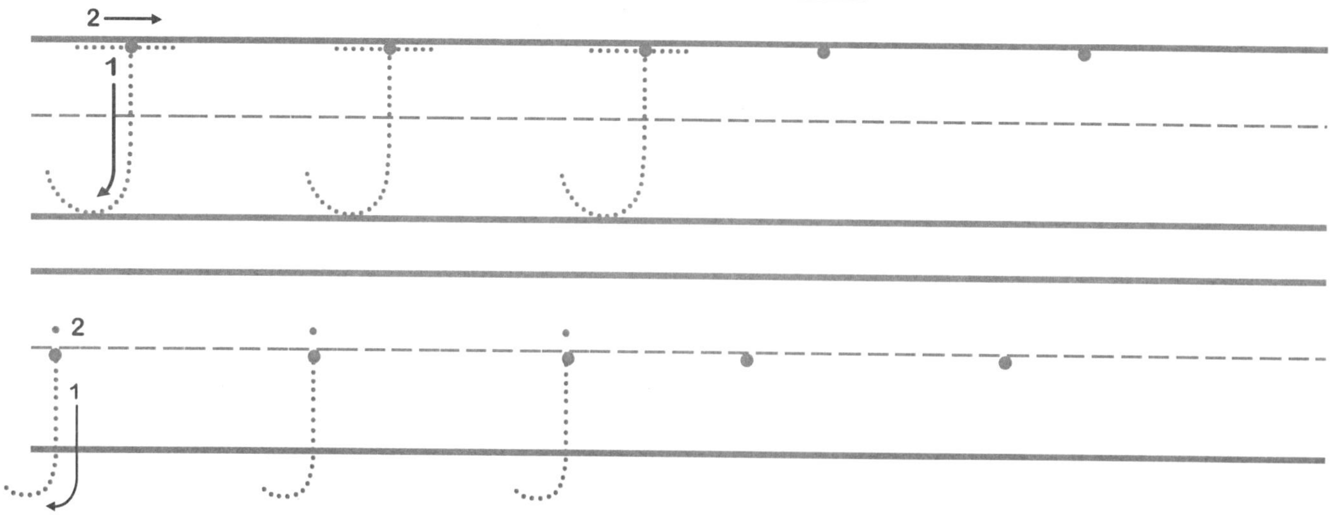

Letter J Practice

Say the name of each object aloud.
Connect "J" to every object that begins with the letter "J."

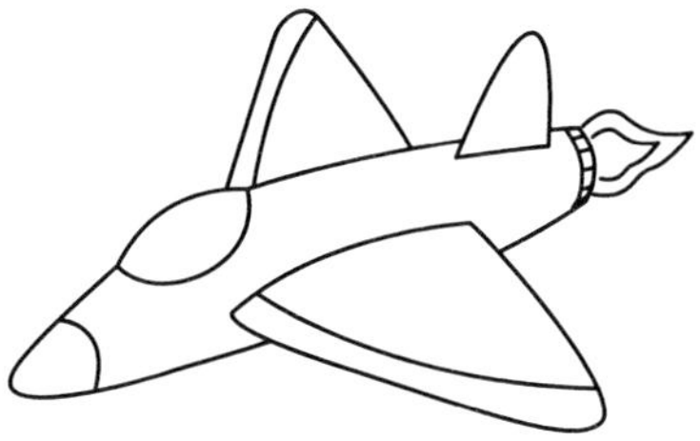

J

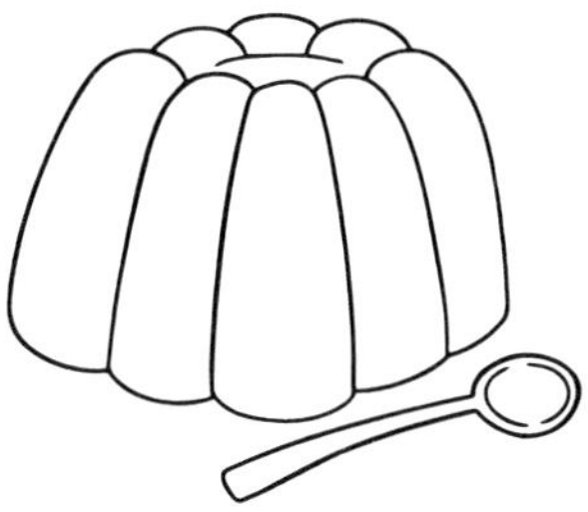

Trace and print the letters on each line.
Circle your best letter on each line.

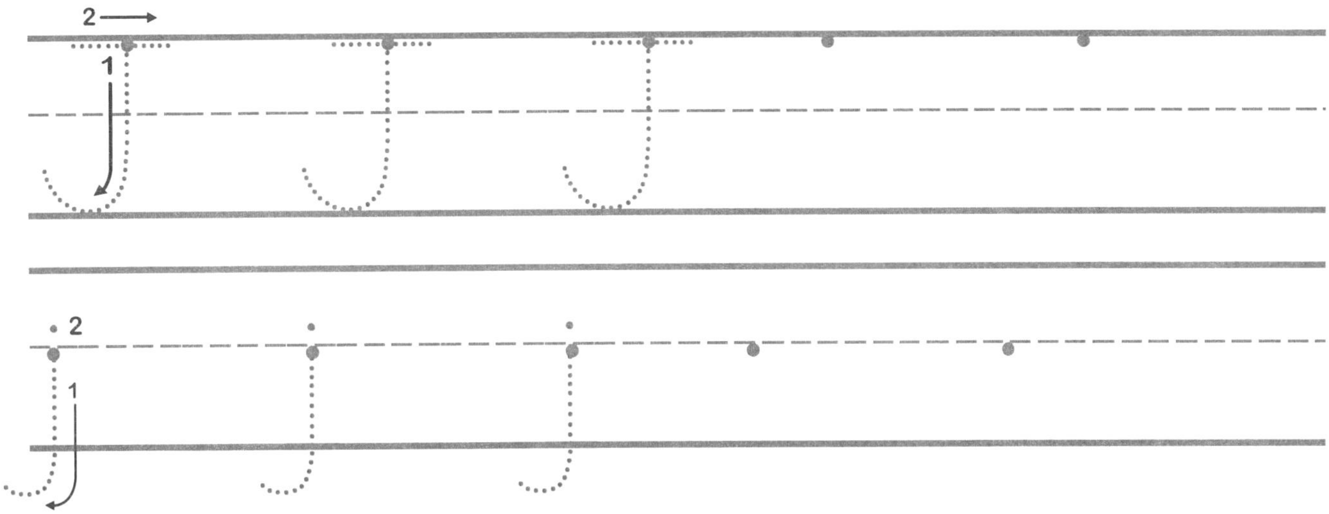

Letter K is for Key

Colour the capital K's. purple
Colour the lowercase k's. green

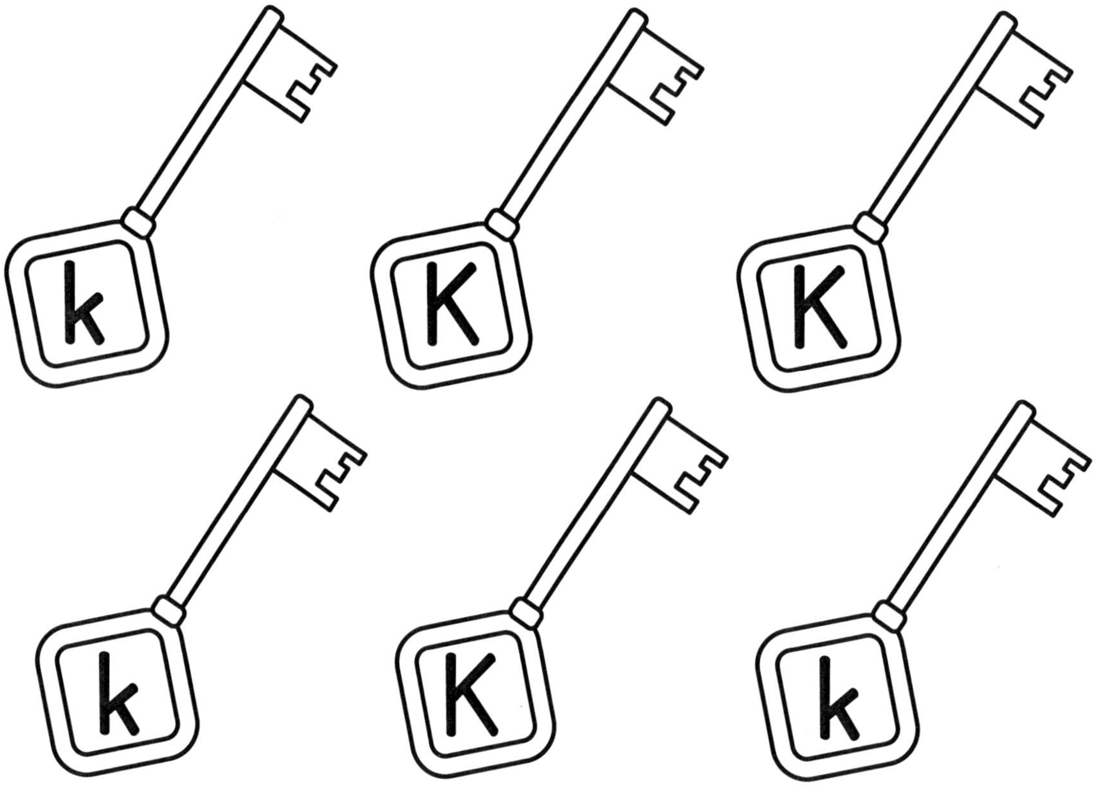

Trace and print the letters on each line.
Circle your best letter on each line.

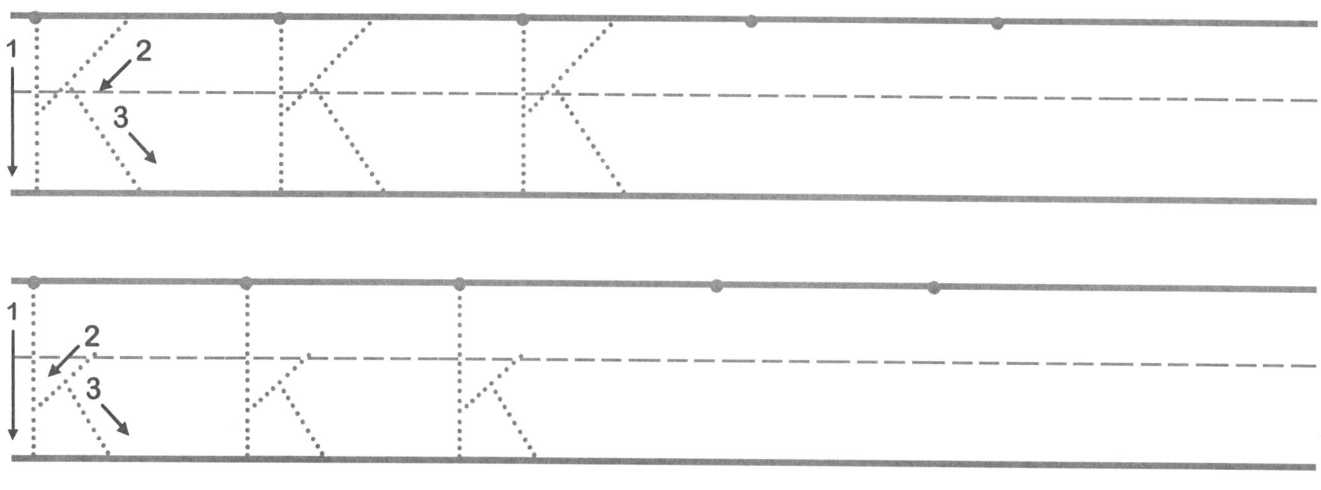

Letter K Practice

Say the name of each object aloud.
Connect “K” to every object that begins with the letter “K.”

K

Trace and print the letters on each line.
Circle your best letter on each line.

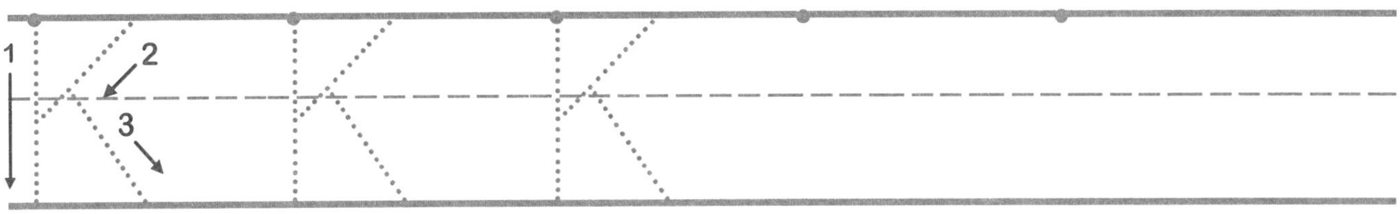

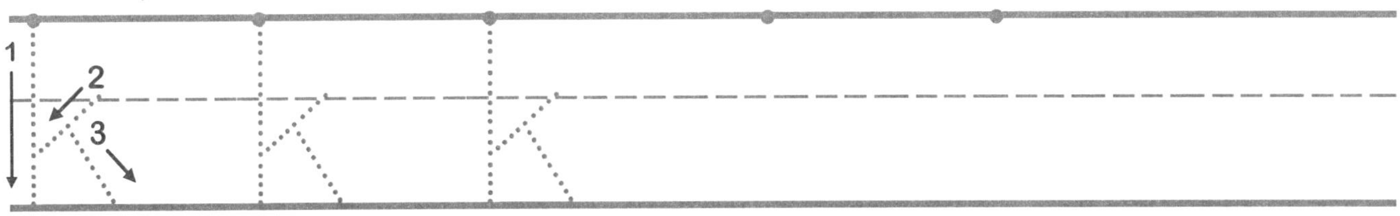

Letter L is for Leaf

Colour the capital L's. blue
Colour the lowercase l's. red

Trace and print the letters on each line.
Circle your best letter on each line.

Letter L Practice

Say the name of each object aloud.
Connect "L" to every object that begins with the letter "L."

L

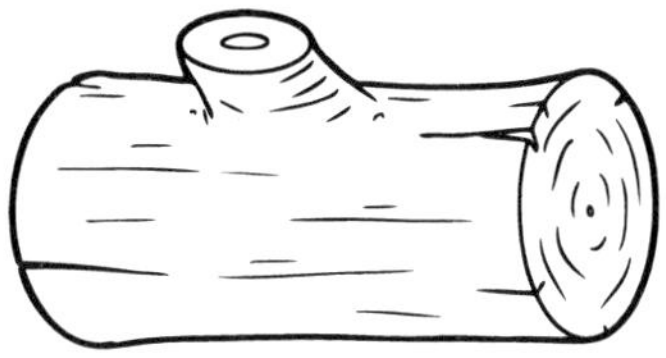

Trace and print the letters on each line.
Circle your best letter on each line.

1

2

1

Letter M is for Mushroom

Colour the capital M's. purple

Colour the lowercase m's. yellow

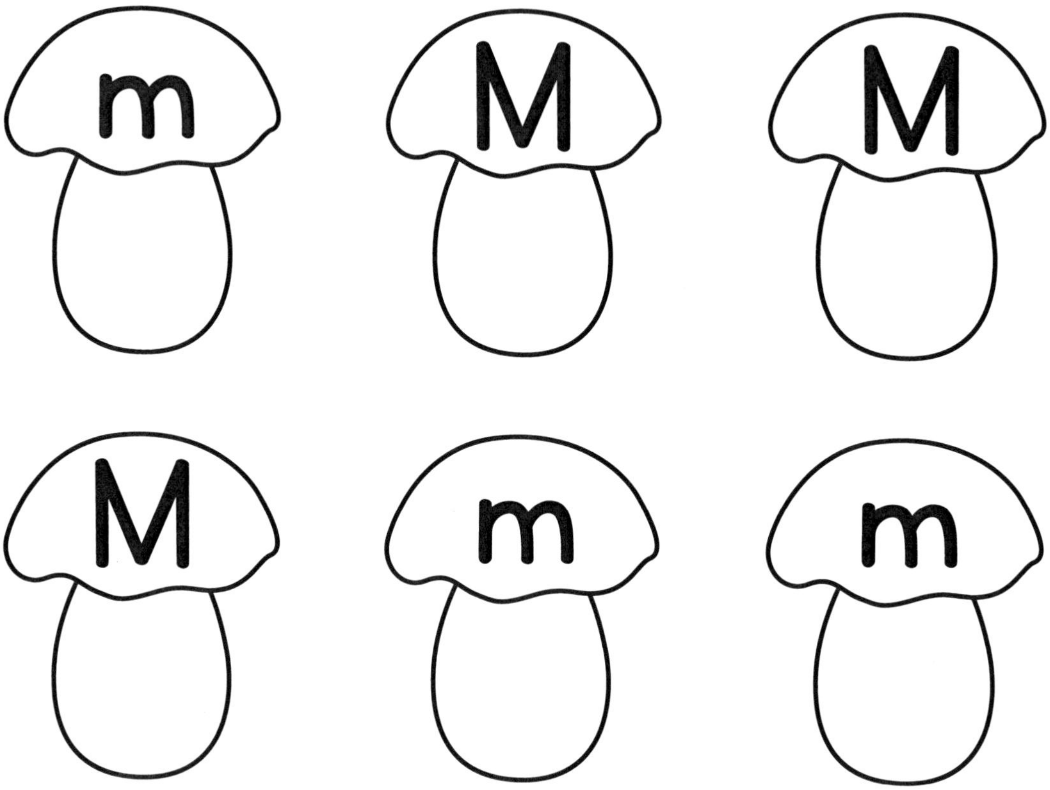

Trace and print the letters on each line.

Circle your best letter on each line.

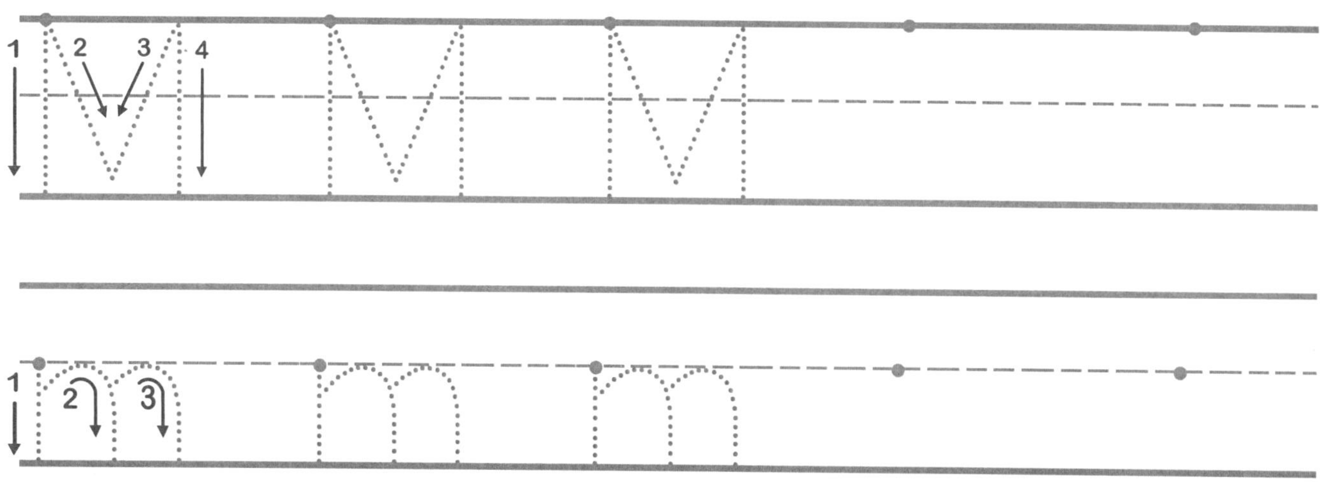

Letter M Practice

Say the name of each object aloud.
Connect "M" to every object that begins with the letter "M."

M

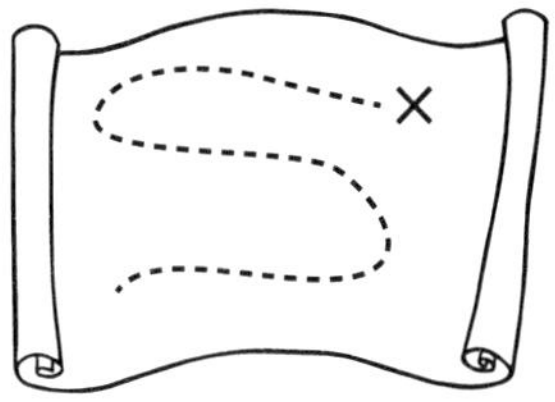

Trace and print the letters on each line.
Circle your best letter on each line.

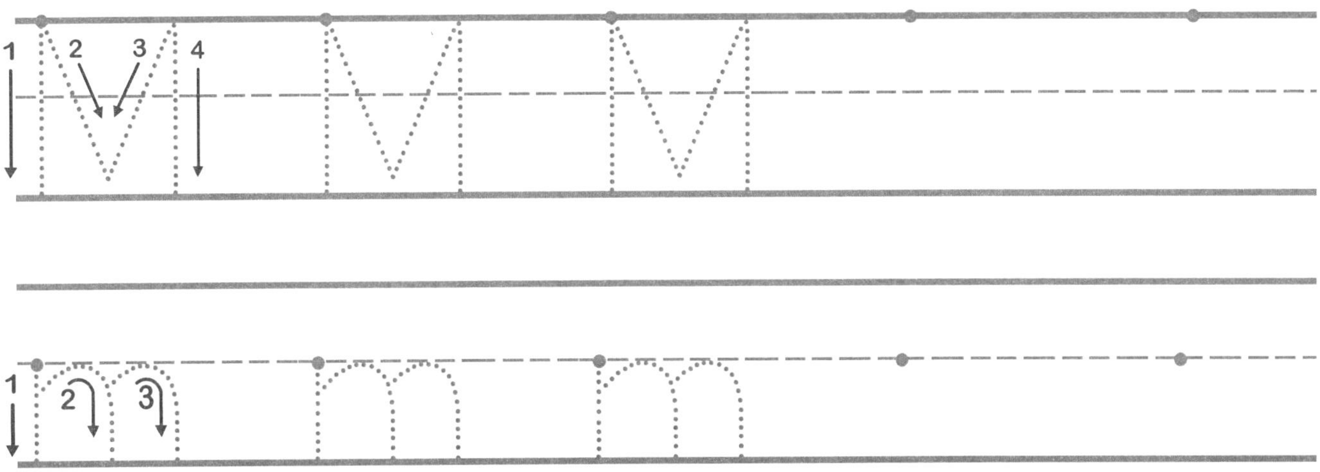

Letter N is for Nut

Colour the capital N's. blue
Colour the lowercase n's. red

Trace and print the letters on each line.
Circle your best letter on each line.

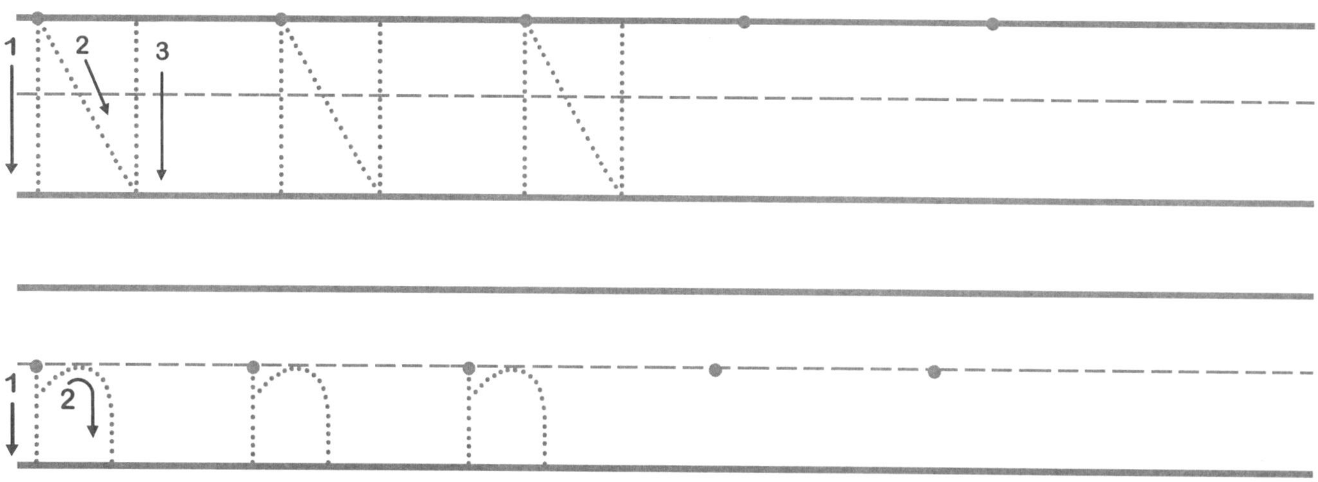

Letter N Practice

Say the name of each object aloud.
Connect "N" to every object that begins with the letter "N."

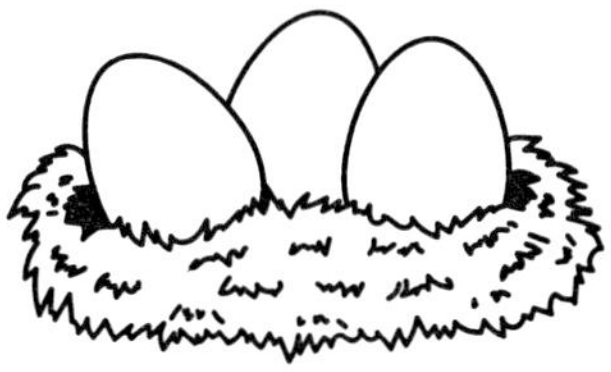

N

Trace and print the letters on each line.
Circle your best letter on each line.

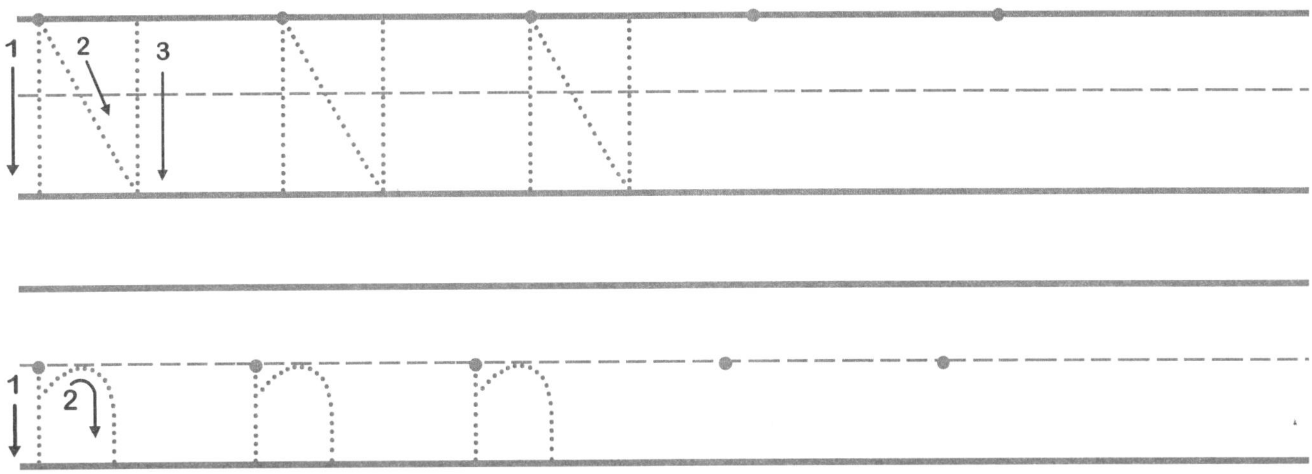

Letter O is for Onion

Colour the capital O's. green

Colour the lowercase o's. orange

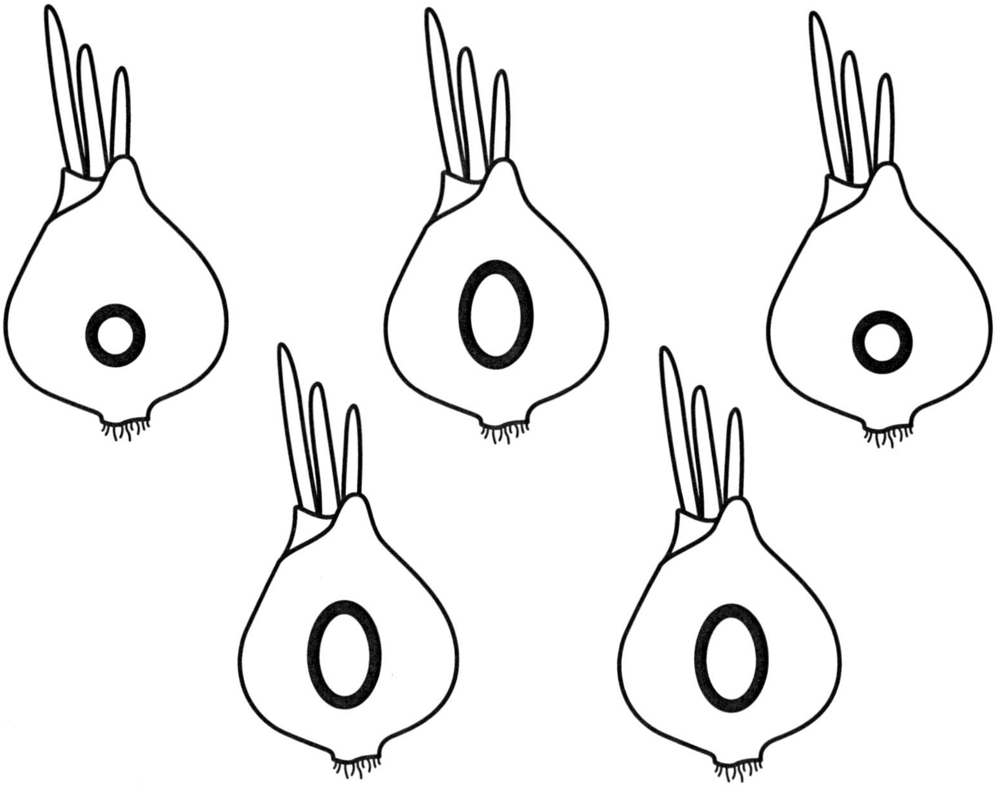

Trace and print the letters on each line.

Circle your best letter on each line.

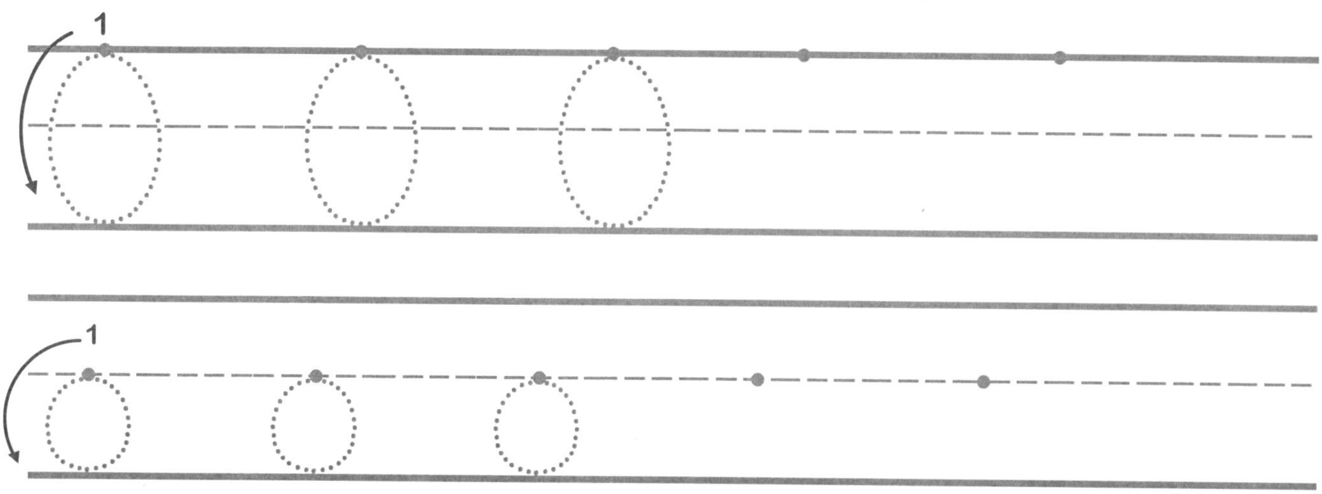

Letter O Practice

Say the name of each object aloud.
Connect "O" to every object that begins with the letter "O."

O

Trace and print the letters on each line.
Circle your best letter on each line.

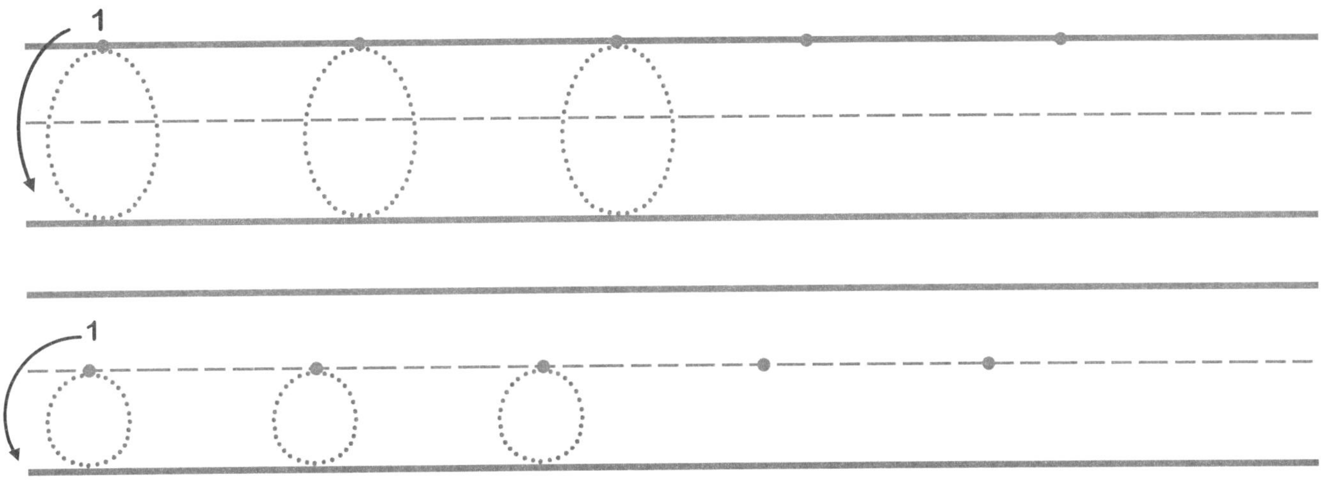

Letter P is for Pepper

Colour the capital P's. orange
Colour the lowercase p's. green

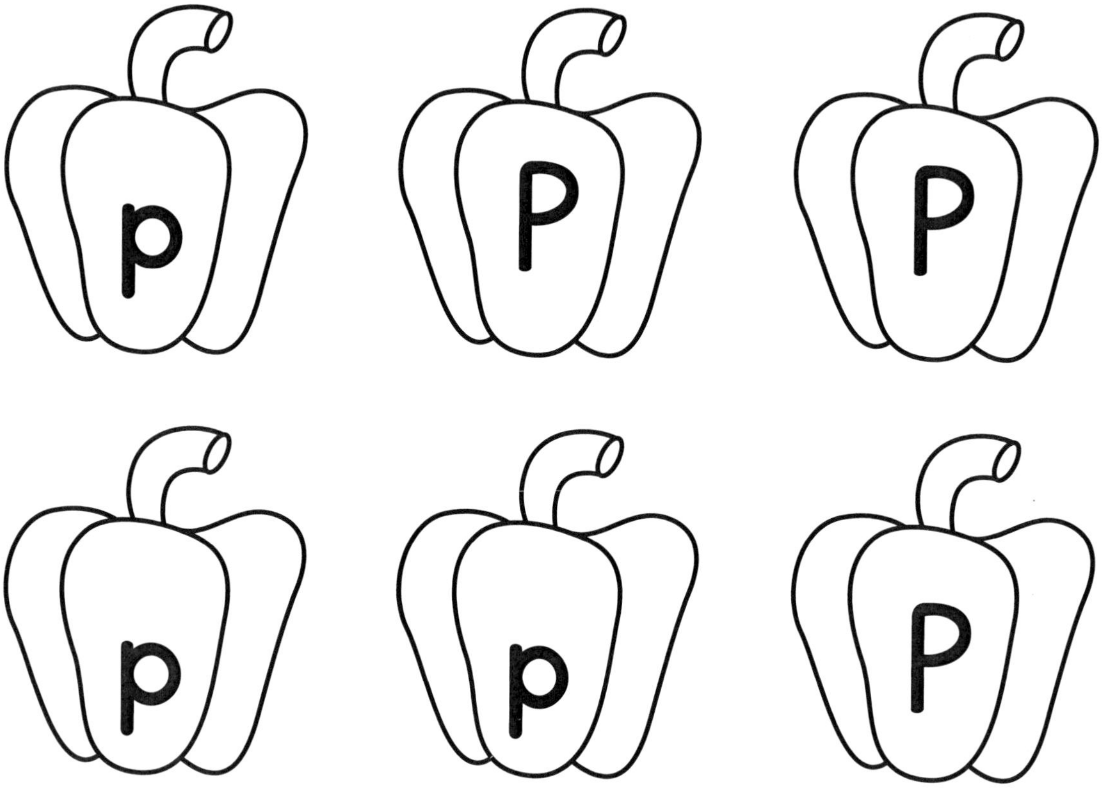

Trace and print the letters on each line.
Circle your best letter on each line.

2
1
P P P

2
1
p p p

Letter P Practice

Say the name of each object aloud.
Connect "P" to every object that begins with the letter "P."

P

Trace and print the letters on each line.
Circle your best letter on each line.

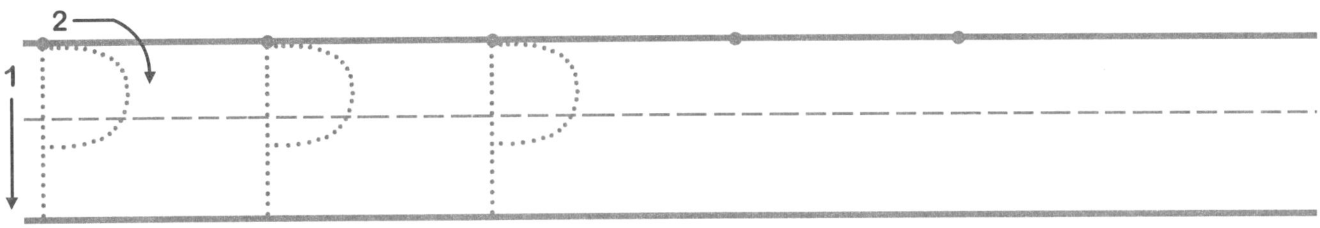

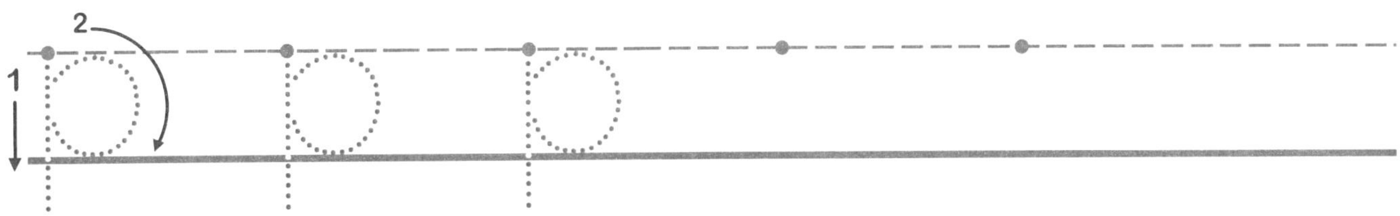

Letter Q is for Quill

Colour the capital Q's. blue
Colour the lowercase q's. red

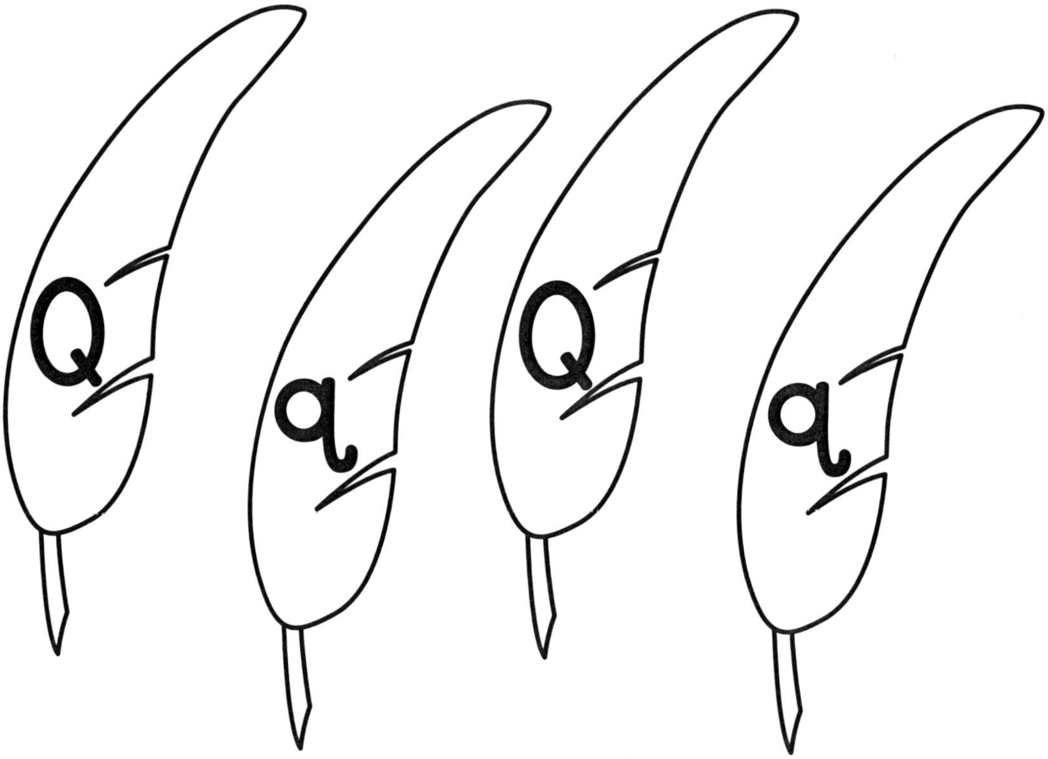

Trace and print the letters on each line.
Circle your best letter on each line.

Letter Q Practice

Say the name of each object aloud.
Connect "Q" to every object that begins with the letter "Q."

Q

Trace and print the letters on each line.
Circle your best letter on each line.

Letter R is for Radish

Colour the capital R's. yellow
Colour the lowercase r's. blue

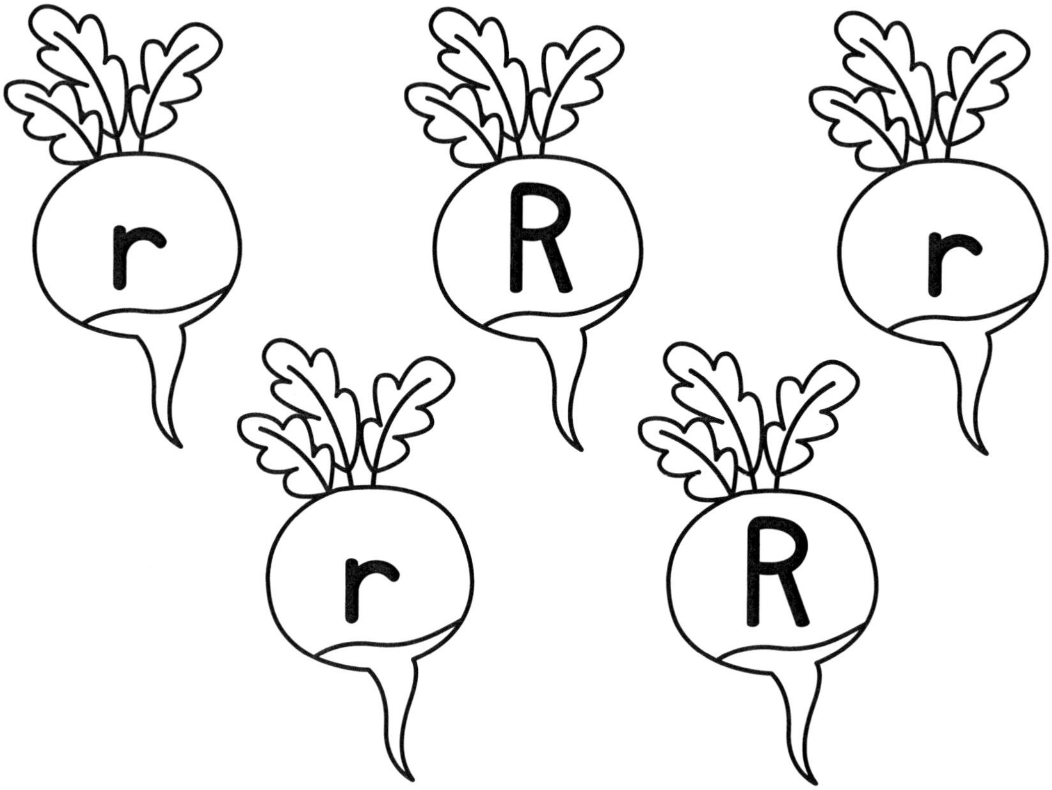

Trace and print the letters on each line.
Circle your best letter on each line.

R R R

r r r

Letter R Practice

Say the name of each object aloud.
Connect "R" to every object that begins with the letter "R."

R

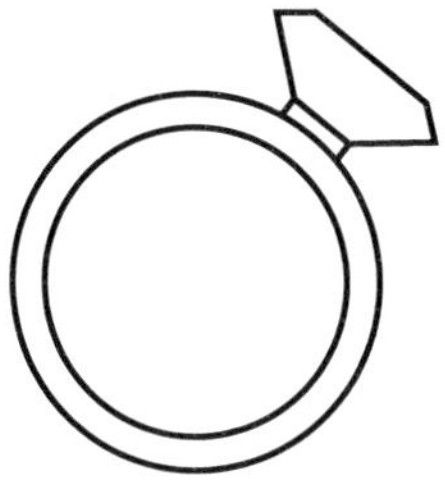

Trace and print the letters on each line.
Circle your best letter on each line.

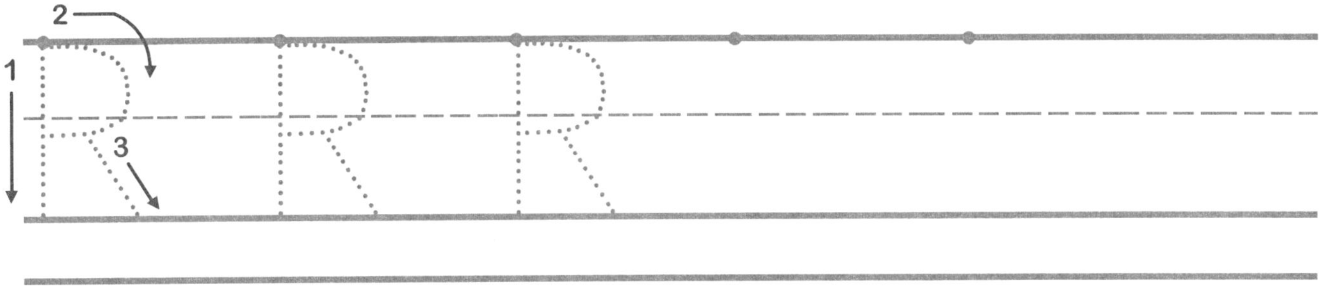

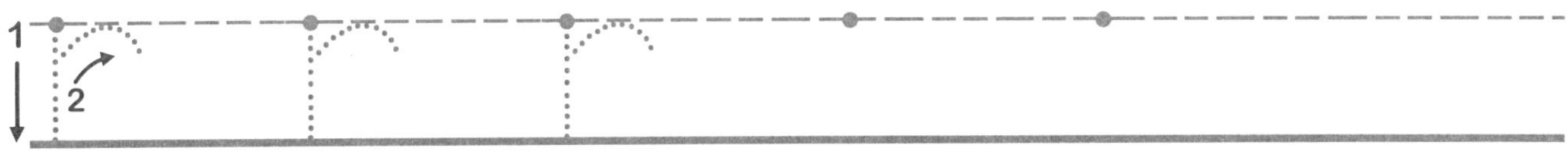

Letter S is for Sock

Colour the capital S's. orange
Colour the lowercase s's. purple

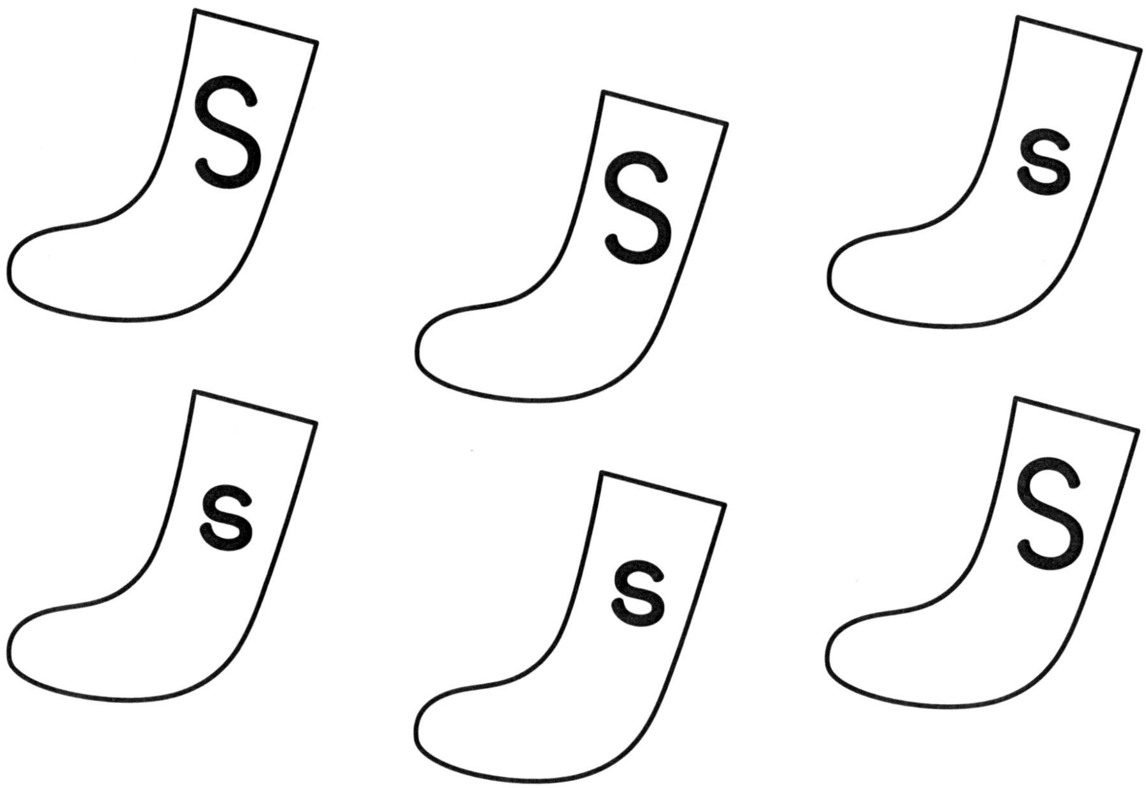

Trace and print the letters on each line.
Circle your best letter on each line.

Letter S Practice

Say the name of each object aloud.
Connect "S" to every object that begins with the letter "S."

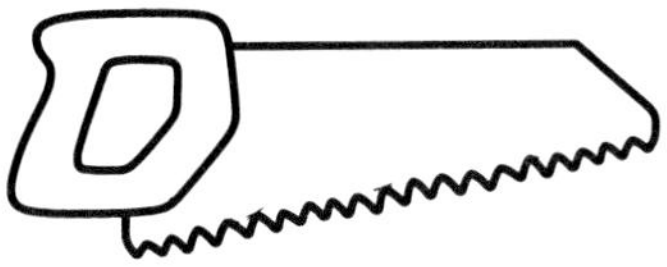

S

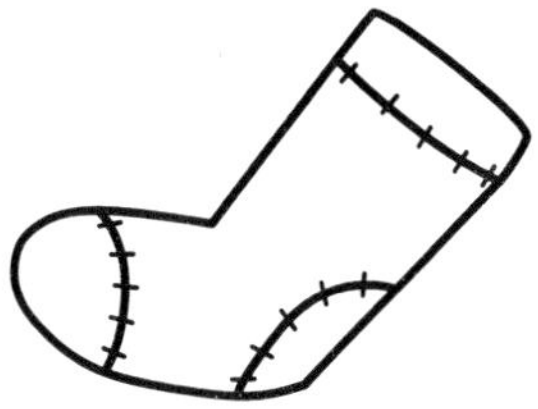

Trace and print the letters on each line.
Circle your best letter on each line.

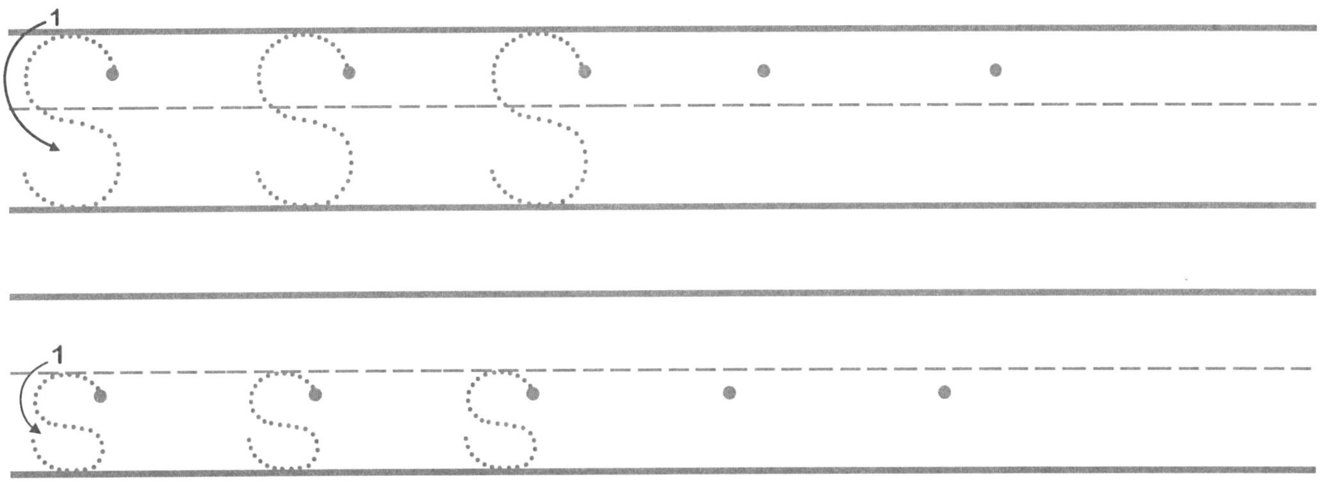

Letter T is for Tomato

Colour the capital T's. blue

Colour the lowercase t's. green

Trace and print the letters on each line.
Circle your best letter on each line.

Letter T Practice

Say the name of each object aloud.
Connect "T" to every object that begins with the letter "T."

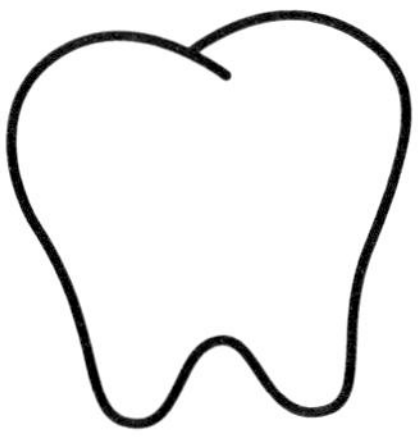

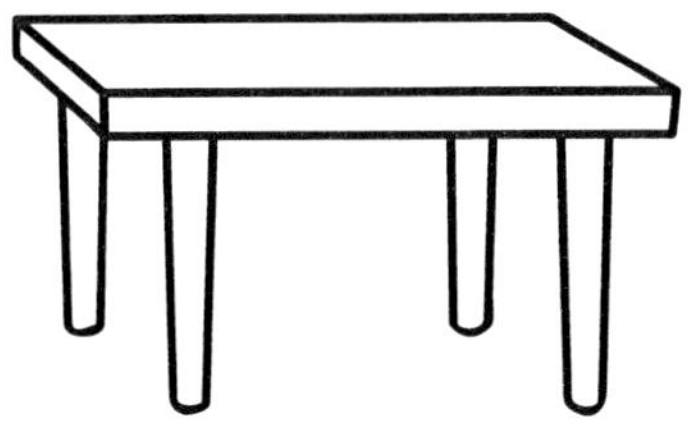

T

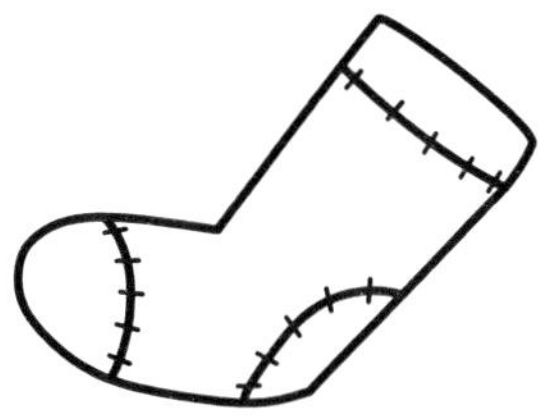

Trace and print the letters on each line.
Circle your best letter on each line.

Letter U is for Umbrella

Colour the capital U's. purple
Colour the lowercase u's. blue

Trace and print the letters on each line.
Circle your best letter on each line.

Letter U Practice

Say the name of each object aloud.
Connect "U" to every object that begins with the letter "U."

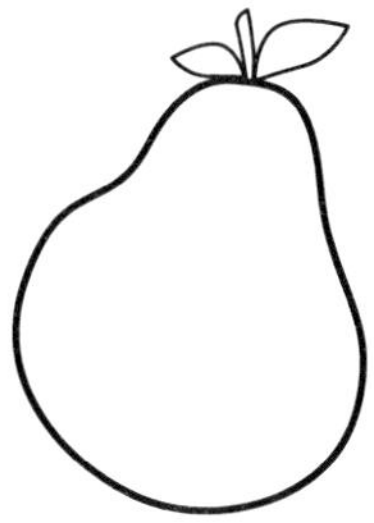

U

Trace and print the letters on each line.
Circle your best letter on each line.

Letter V is for Vase

Colour the capital V's. red
Colour the lowercase v's. green

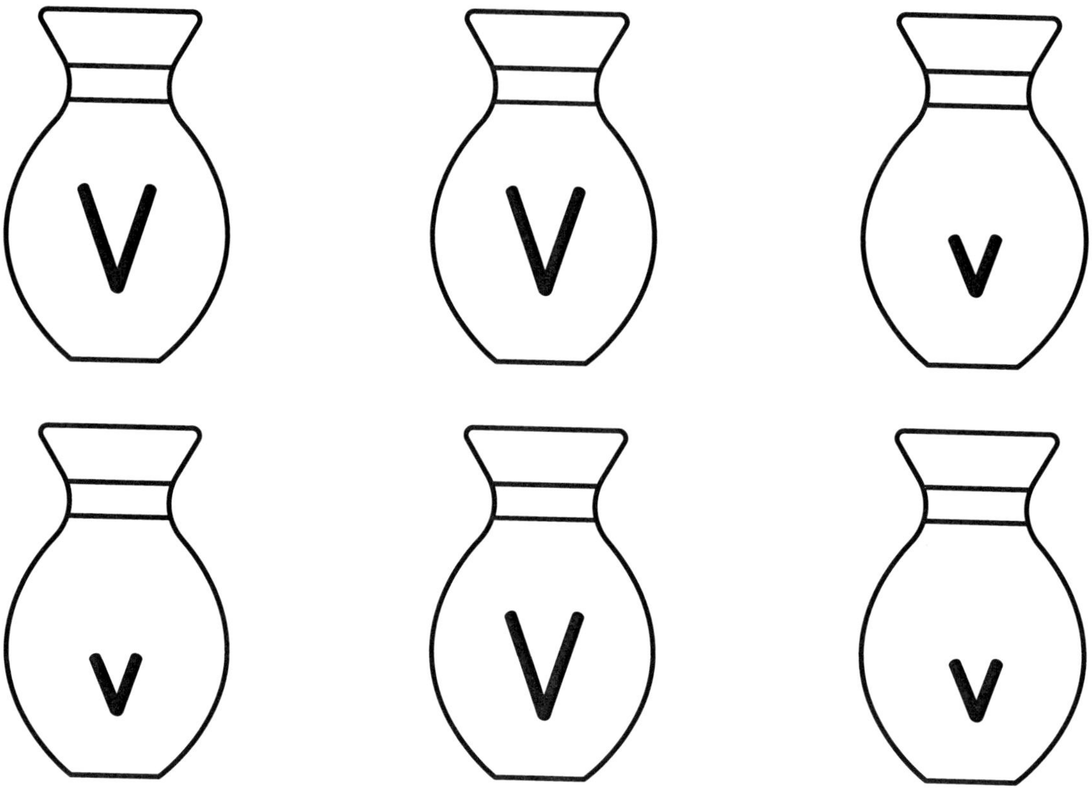

Trace and print the letters on each line.
Circle your best letter on each line.

Letter V Practice

Say the name of each object aloud.
Connect "V" to every object that begins with the letter "V."

V

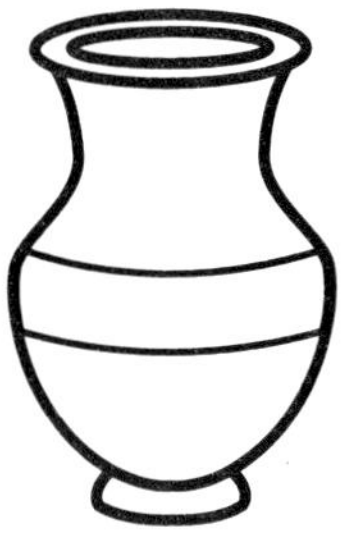

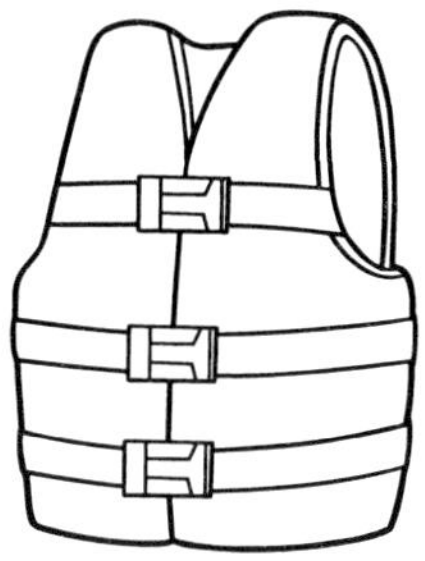

Trace and print the letters on each line.
Circle your best letter on each line.

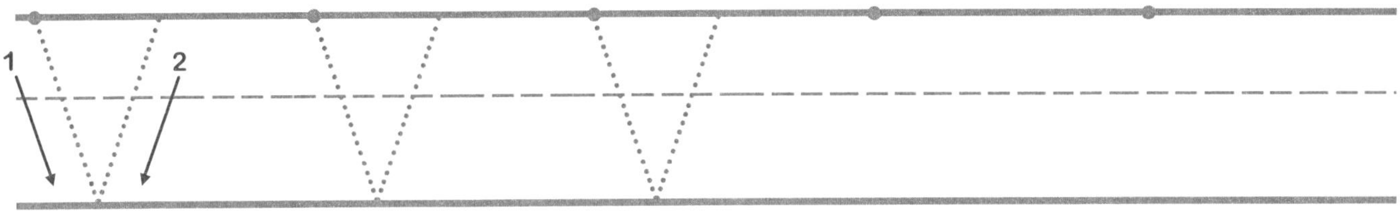

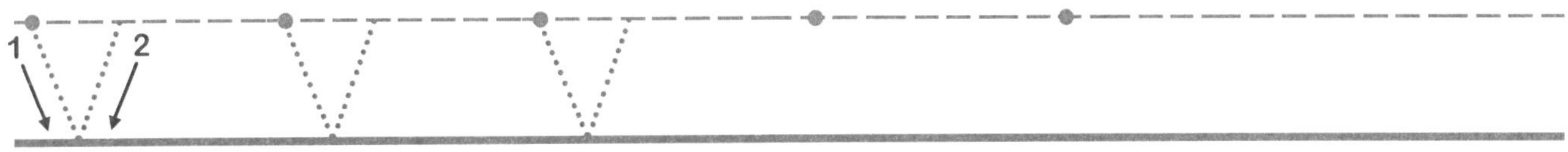

Letter W is for Whistle

Colour the capital W's. blue
Colour the lowercase w's. red

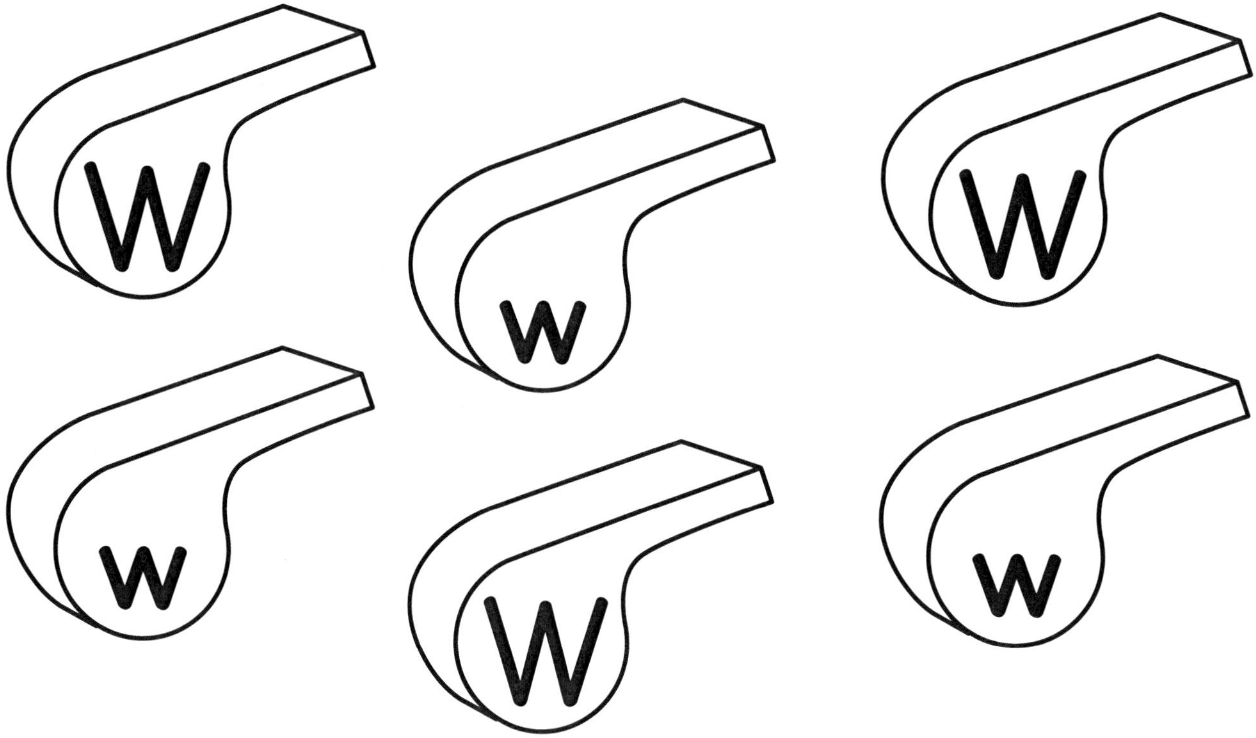

Trace and print the letters on each line.
Circle your best letter on each line.

Letter W Practice

Say the name of each object aloud.
Connect "W" to every object that begins with the letter "W."

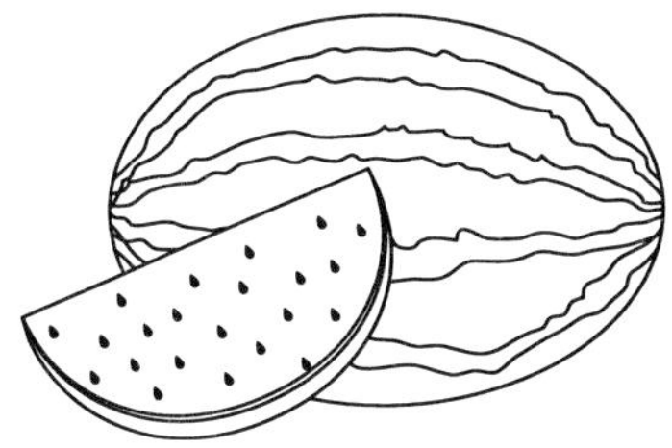

W

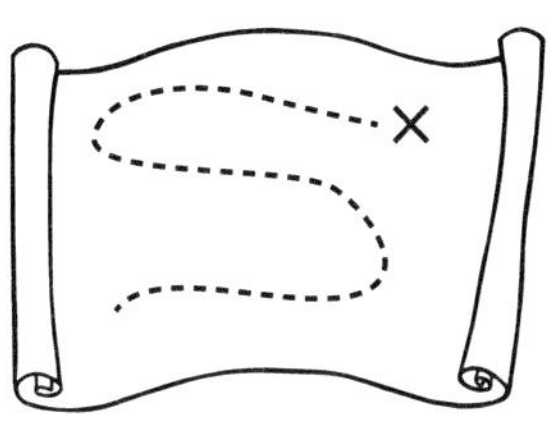

Trace and print the letters on each line.
Circle your best letter on each line.

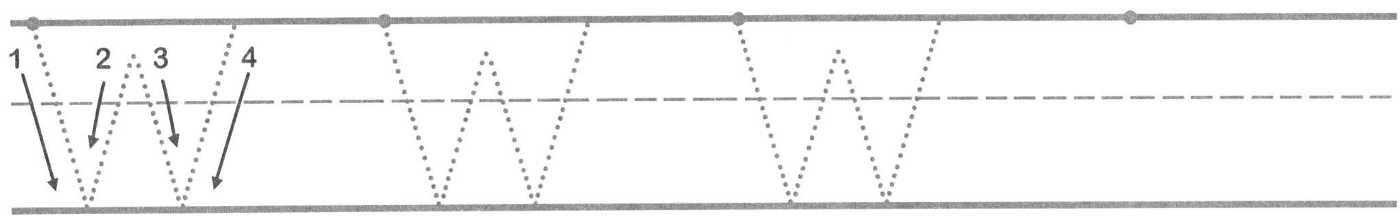

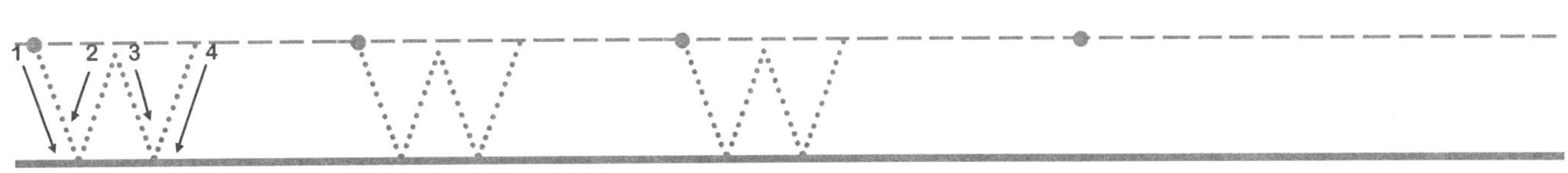

Letter X is for Xylophone

Colour the capital X's. yellow
Colour the lowercase x's. blue

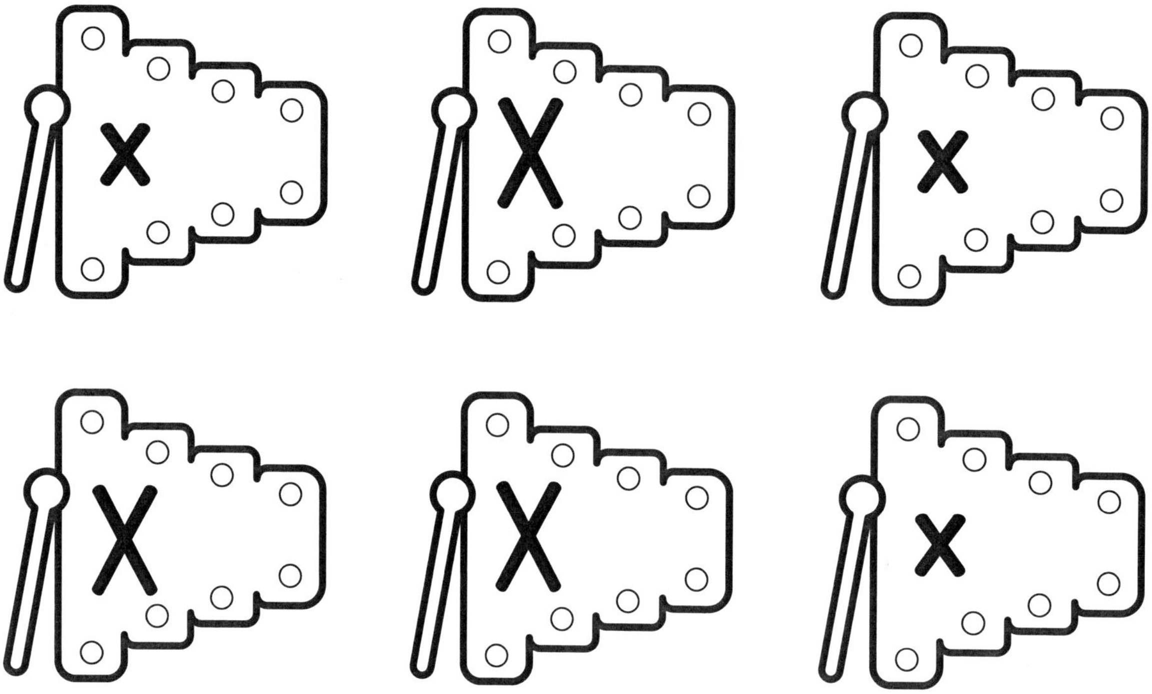

Trace and print the letters on each line.
Circle your best letter on each line.

1 X 2 X X

1 x 2 x x

Letter X Practice

Say the name of each object aloud.
Connect "X" to every object that begins with the letter "X."

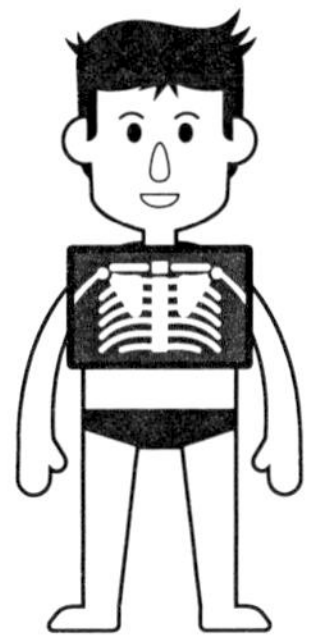

X

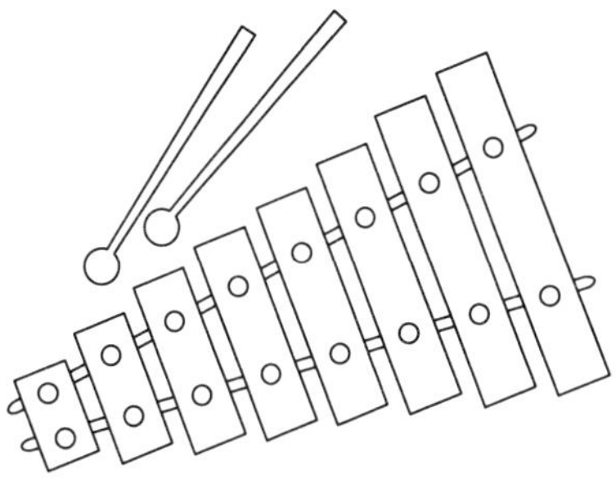

Trace and print the letters on each line.
Circle your best letter on each line.

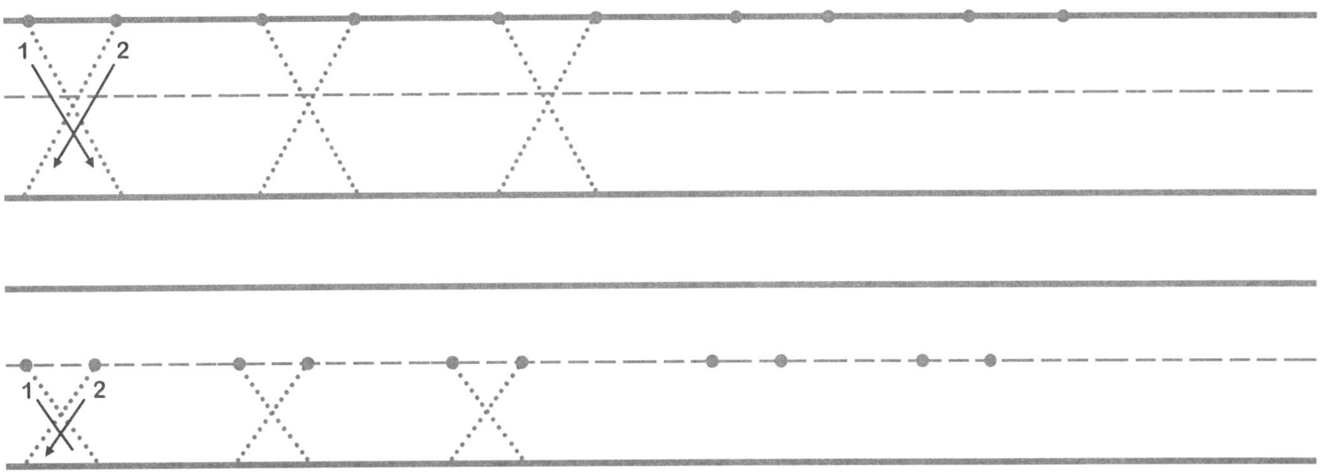

Letter Y is for Yolk

Colour the capital Y's. 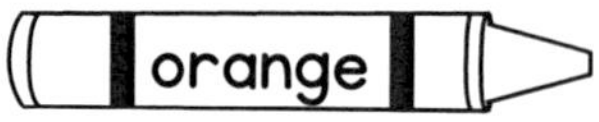

Colour the lowercase y's. 

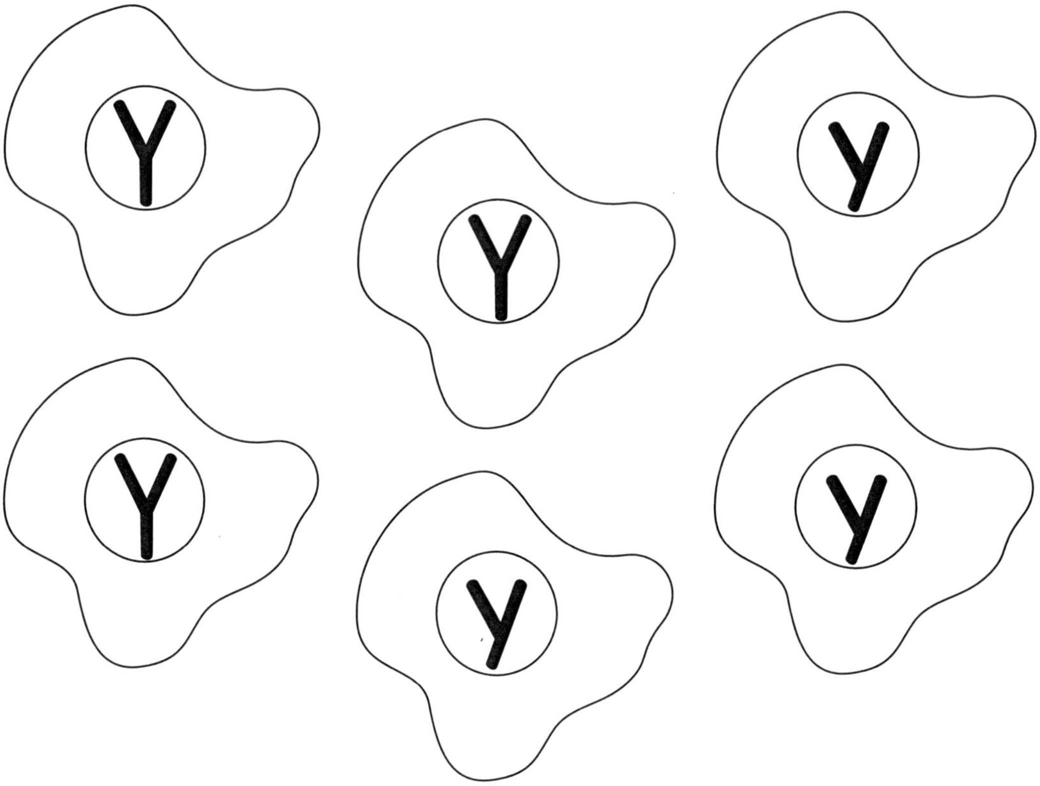

Trace and print the letters on each line.
Circle your best letter on each line.

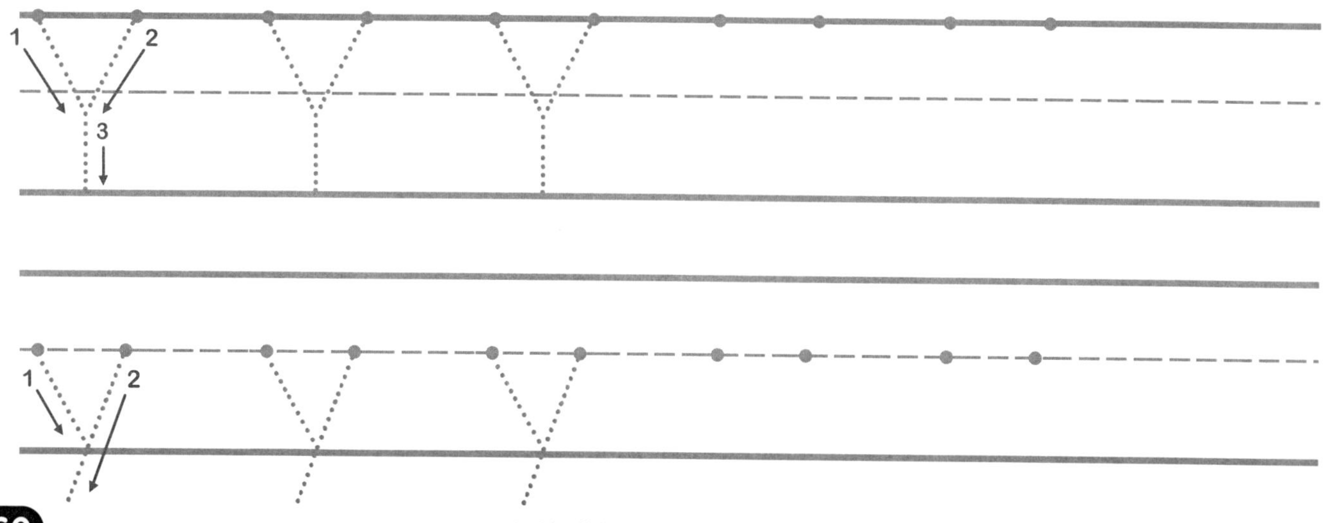

Letter Y Practice

Say the name of each object aloud.
Connect "Y" to every object that begins with the letter "Y."

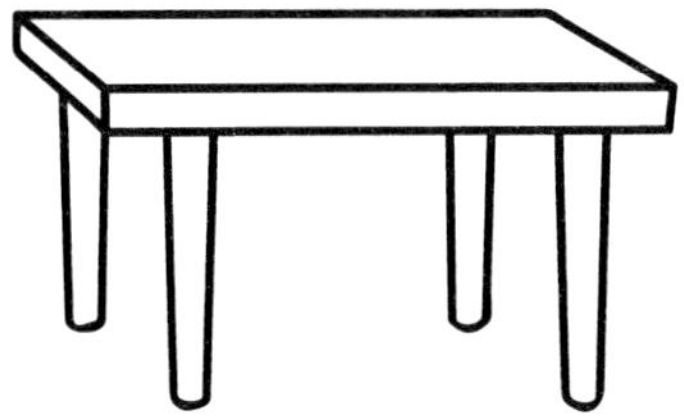

Y

Trace and print the letters on each line.
Circle your best letter on each line.

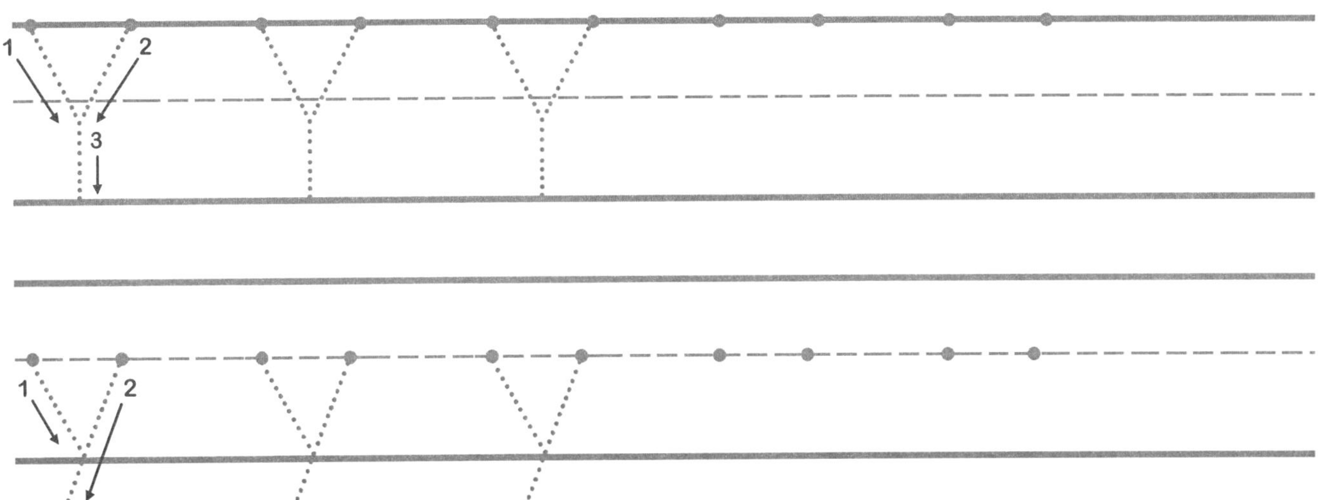

Letter Z is for Zuchinni

Colour the capital Z's. green

Colour the lowercase z's. blue

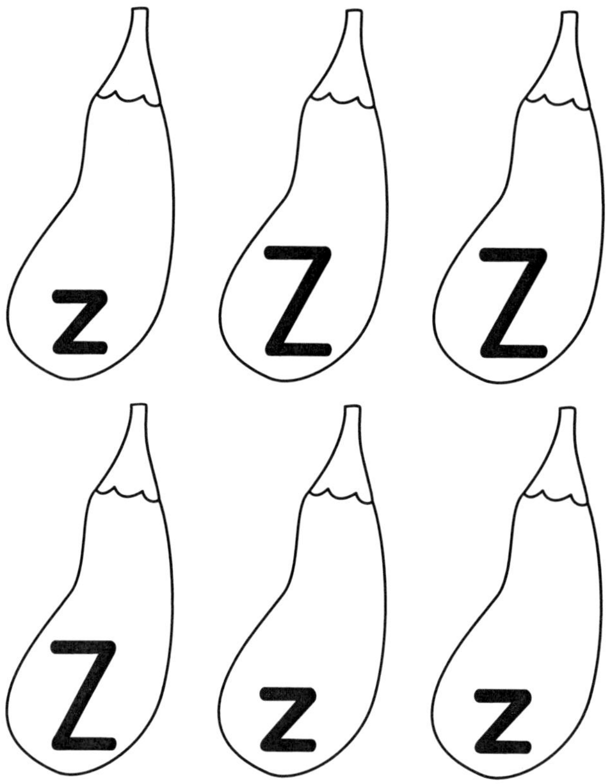

Trace and print the letters on each line.

Circle your best letter on each line.

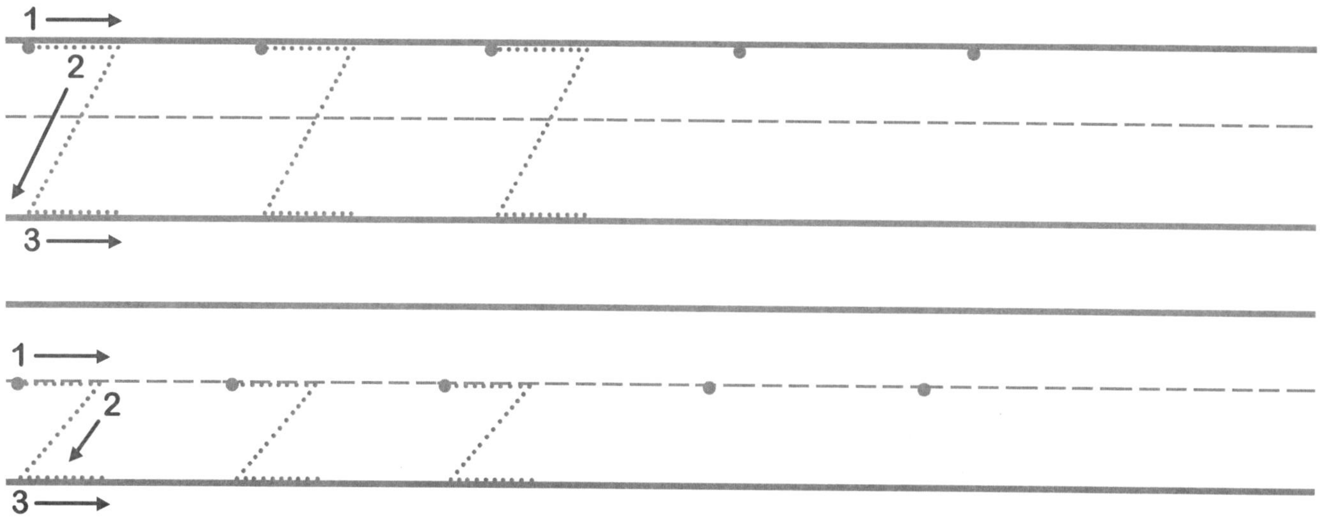

Letter Z Practice

Say the name of each object aloud.
Connect "Z" to every object that begins with the letter "Z."

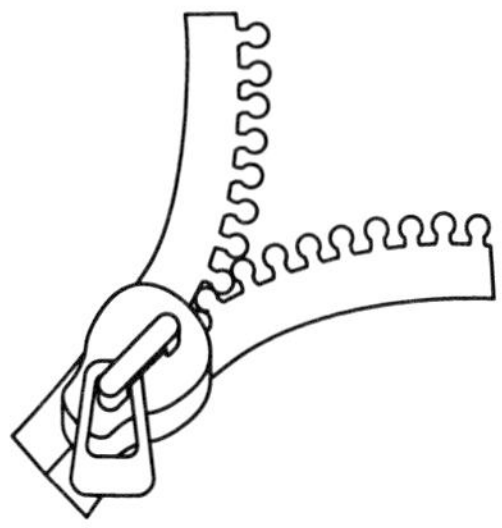

Z

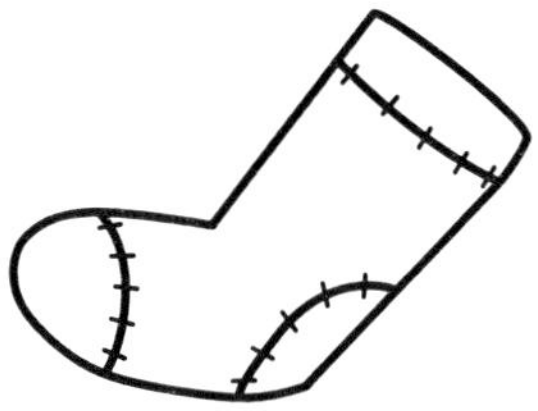

Trace and print the letters on each line.
Circle your best letter on each line.

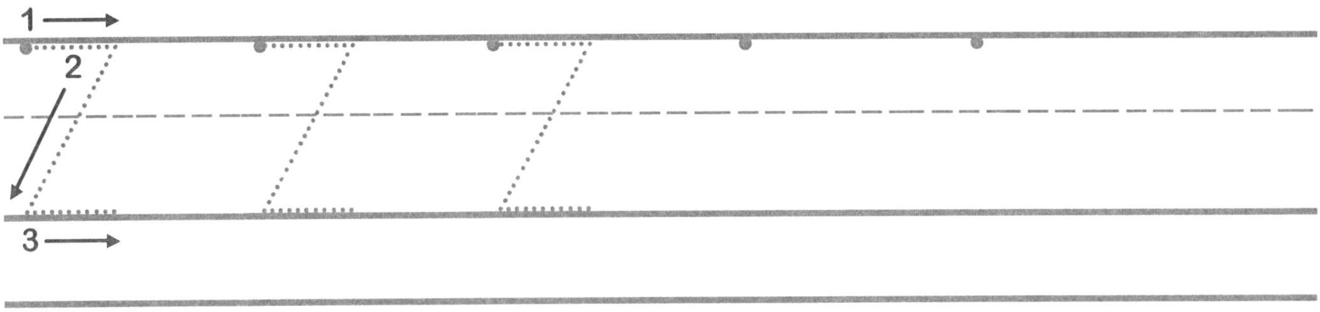

Alphabet Fun

Fill in the missing uppercase letters of the alphabet.
Colour the train.

Alphabet Fun

Fill in the missing lowercase letters of the alphabet.
Colour the train.

Connect the Dots: A-Z

Connect the dots following A-Z.

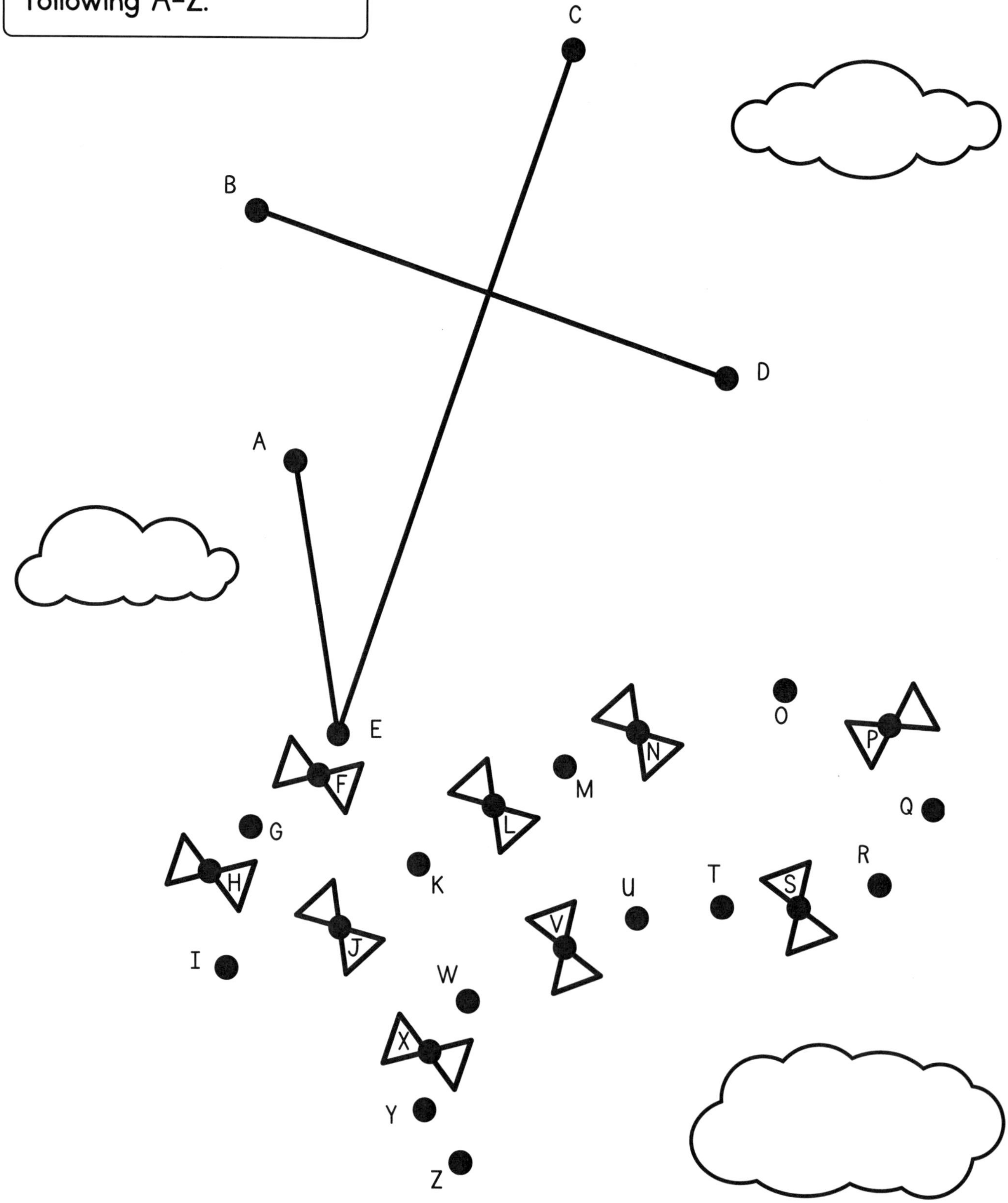

Beginning and Ending Letter Sounds

Circle the Beginning Sound

Say the name of the object out loud. Circle the beginning sound for the object. Colour all the objects.

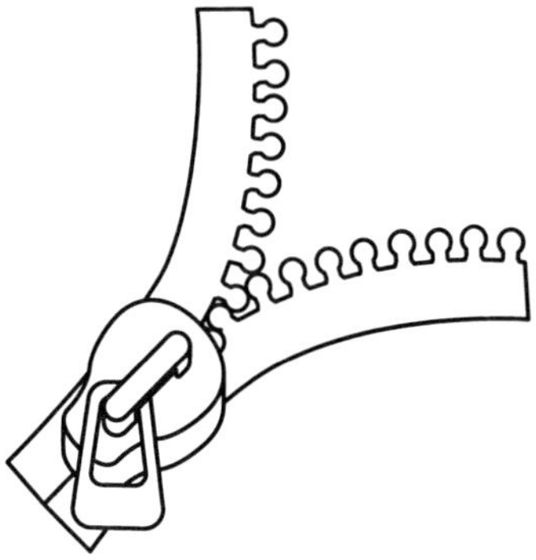

x y z

d e f

s t u

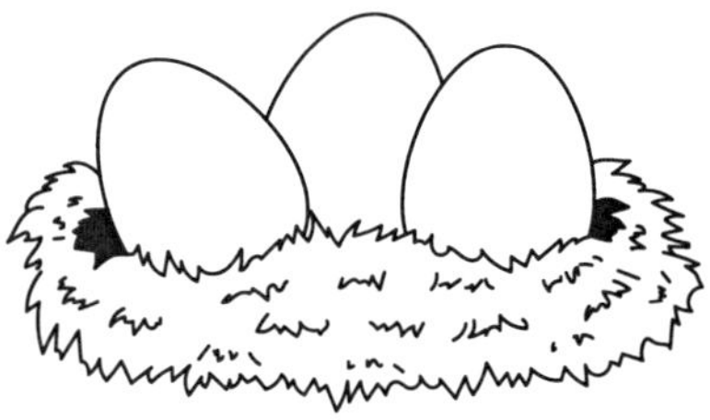

m n o

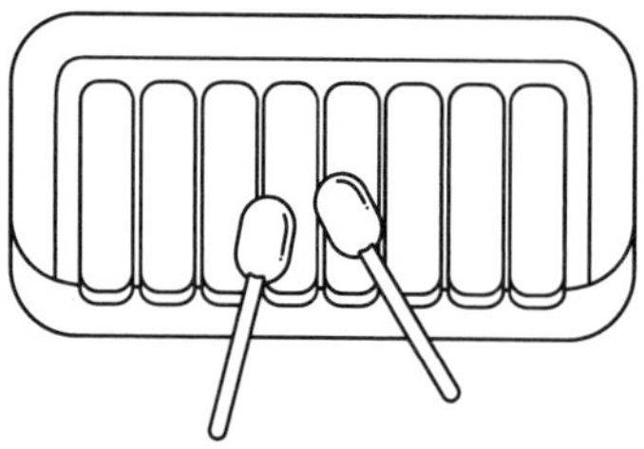

x y z

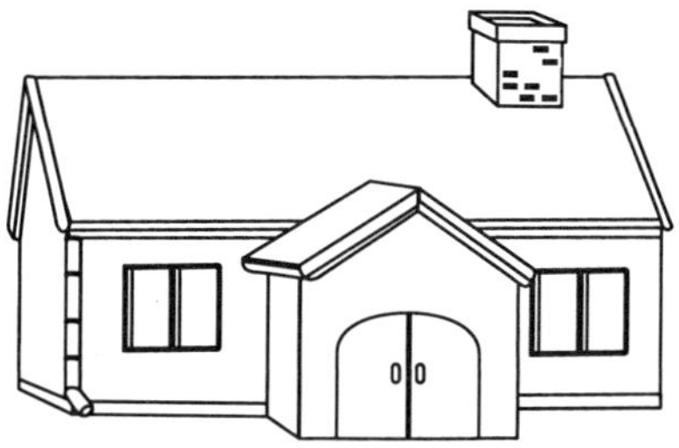

g h i

Colour the zipper.	blue	Colour the nest.	brown
Colour the fish.	green	Colour the xylophone.	yellow
Colour the umbrella.	red	Colour the house.	purple

Circle the Beginning Sound

Say the name of the object out loud. Circle the beginning sound for the object. Colour all the objects.

j k l

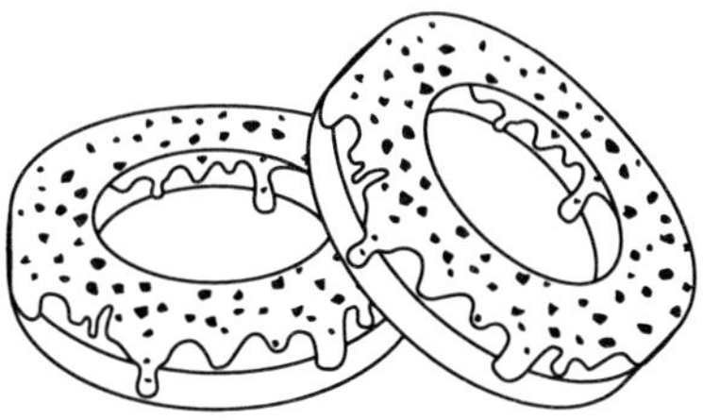

d e f

s t y

j k l

q r s

a b c

Colour the koala.	orange	Colour the ladybug.	red
Colour the doughnut.	green	Colour the queen.	purple
Colour the sun.	yellow	Colour the butterfly.	blue

Identifying Beginning Sounds

Say the name of each object out loud. Print the letter that is the beginning sound for the object.

__og

__at

__ug

__at

__ig

__en

Colour the dog.	blue	Colour the cat.	yellow
Colour the bat.	green	Colour the pig.	purple
Colour the bug.	red	Colour the hen.	orange

Identifying Beginning Sounds

Say the name of each object out loud. Fill in the missing beginning letter from the letters on the right. Then cross out the letter.

Picture	Word	Letters
	_oo	k
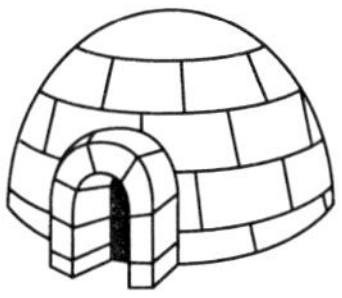	_gloo	o
	_ree	z
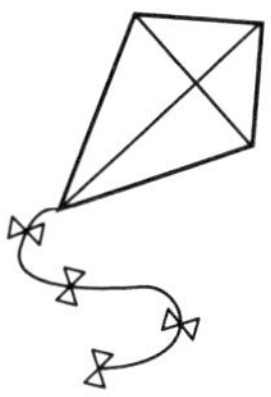	_ite	t
	_wl	i

Beginning Letter Sounds

Change the letter that makes the beginning sound. The new word is the object in the picture. Print the new word on the line.

Change **cat** to 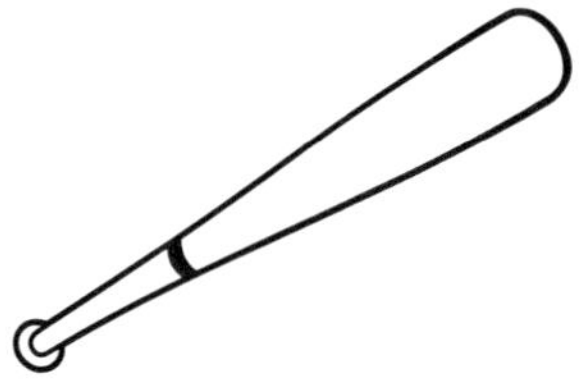 ____________

Change **fun** to  ____________

Change **hot** to  ____________

Change **dog** to  ____________

Change **pen** to  ____________

Beginning Letter Sounds

Circle the objects that have the same beginning sound as the word.
Colour in the pictures.

van

fan

dog

man

pen

Colour the Ending Sound

Look at the picture. Say the name of the object out loud.
Colour in the ending sound for the object.

 n t	 g t
 v g	 u t
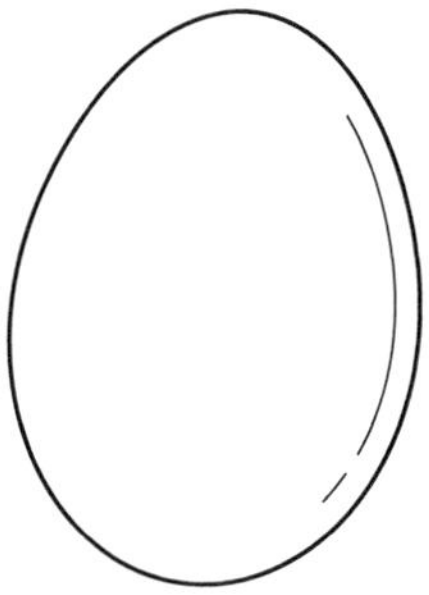 u g	 f r
 o x	 t m

Colour the Ending Sound

Look at the picture. Say the name of the object out loud.
Colour in the ending sound for the object.

	b f		r n
	z o		a p
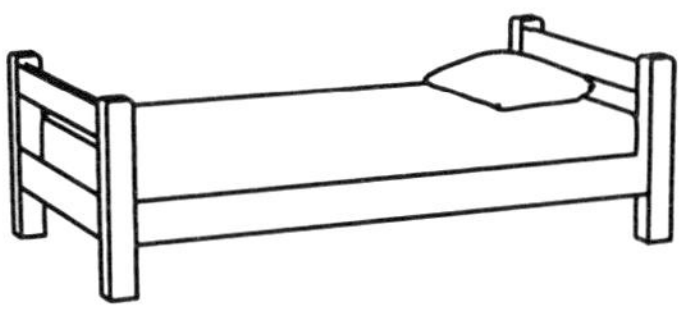	d q		l n
	e t		j m

Ending Letter Sounds

Circle the objects that have the same ending sound as the word.
Colour in the objects.

sled

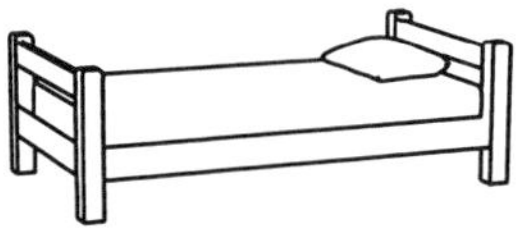

wig

wall

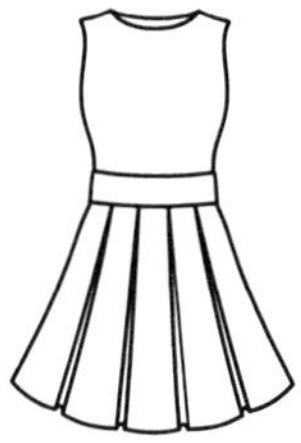

ox

pup

Ending Letter Sounds

Say the name of each object out loud. Fill in the missing ending letter from the letters on the right. Then cross out the letter.

fro

r

ja

w

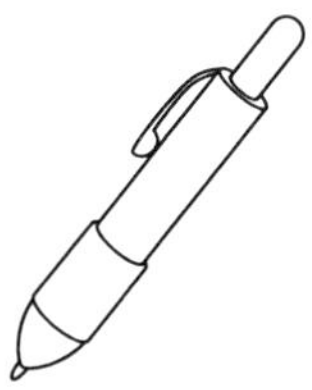

pe

l

wel

g

co

n

Ending Letter Sounds

Say the name of each object out loud at the beginning of each row. Circle the ending letter sound for each object.

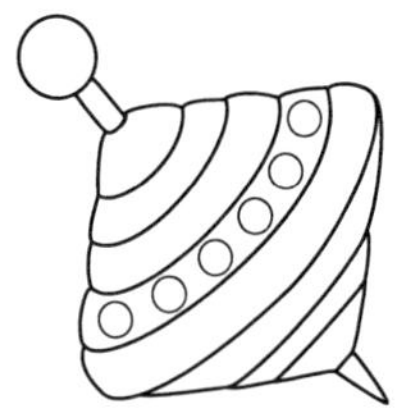

r m p

s y x

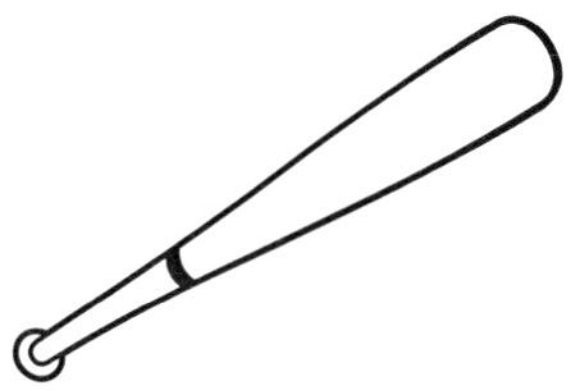

s t w

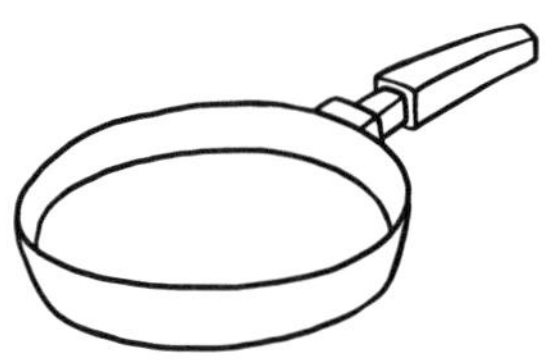

v n r

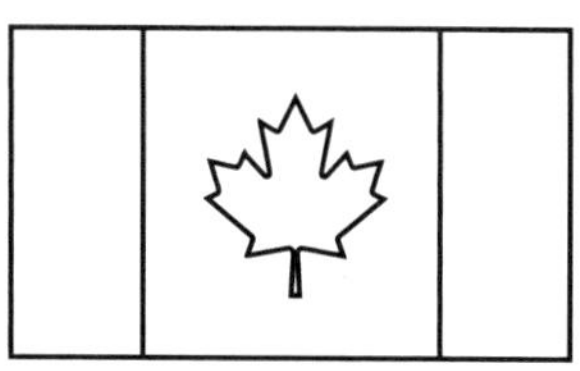

p h g

Ending Letter Sounds

Say the name of each object out loud. Print the letter that is the ending letter sound for the object.

boo__

ca__

bir__

bo__

tu__

ca__

Colour the book. red
Colour the cat. yellow
Colour the bird. blue

Colour the box. brown
Colour the tub. purple
Colour the car. orange

Beginning and Ending Letter Sounds

Say the name of the object out loud. Complete the word by adding the beginning and ending sound letters.

__ e __

__ o __

__ u __

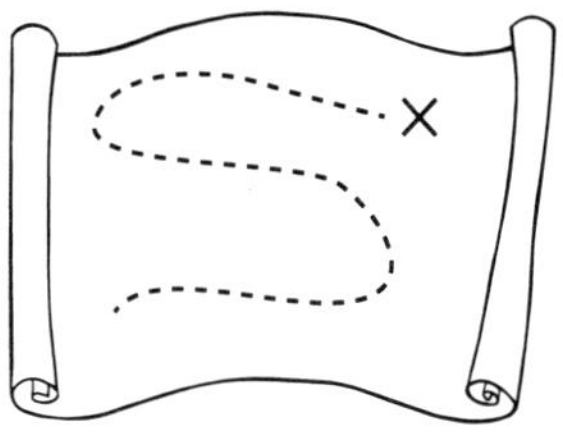

__ a __

__ o __

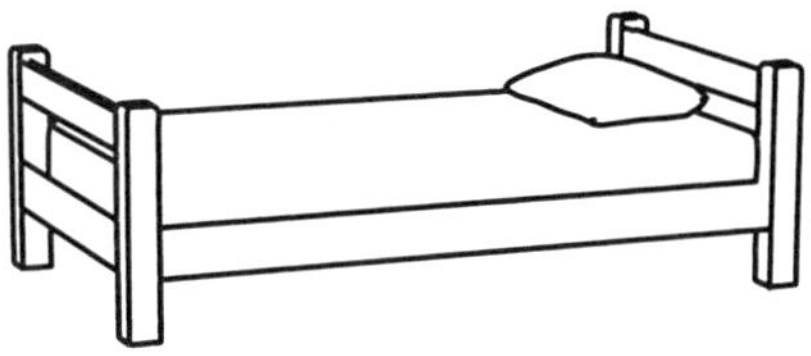

__ e __

Beginning and Ending Letter Sounds

Say the name of the object out loud. Complete the word by adding the beginning and ending sound letters.

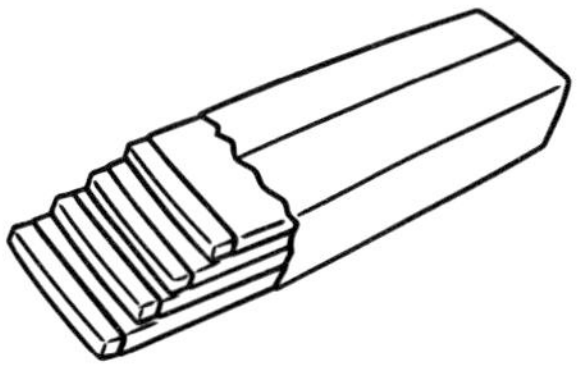

u

o

e

i

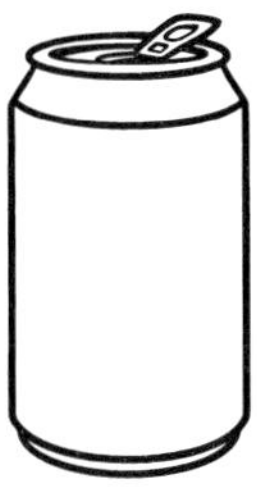

a

u

Short and Long Vowel Sounds

Short and Long Vowel Sounds

Long vowels say their own name. Short vowels make different sounds. Read the examples below, say the name of the object out loud.

a

short ă  jam

long ā  cave

e

short ĕ 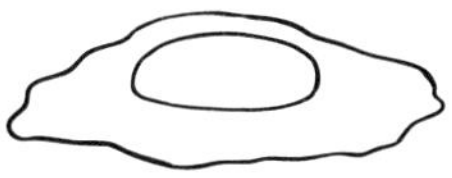 egg

long ē  bee

i

short ĭ 

milk

long ī 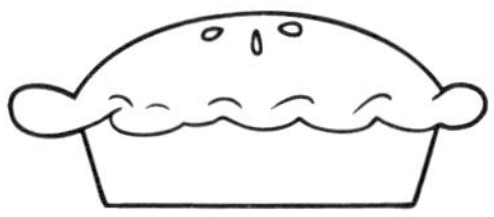 pie

o

short ŏ  top

long ō  globe

u

short ŭ  nut

long ū 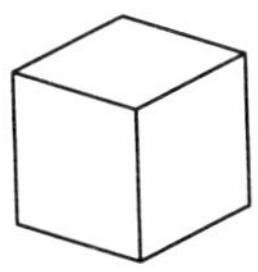 cube

Short a Sound

Say the name of the object out loud.
Fill in the missing vowel for each of the words.

ă

r _ t

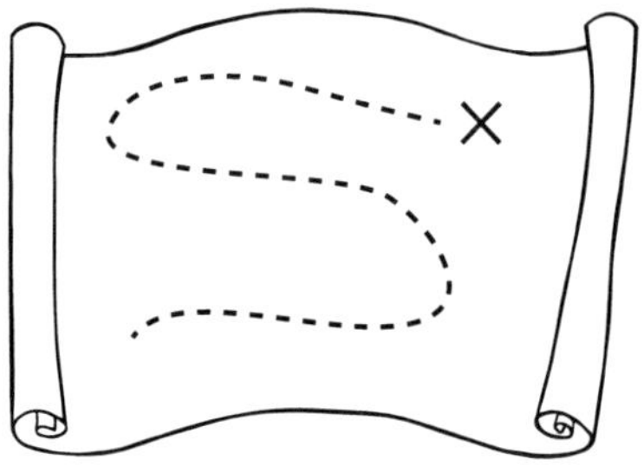

m _ p

f _ n

j _ m

c _ p

c _ b

Colour the rat.	blue
Colour the map.	green
Colour the fan.	red
Colour the jam.	brown
Colour the cap.	purple
Colour the cab.	yellow

Short a Sound

Say the name of the object out loud.
Draw a line to match the object to its word.

map

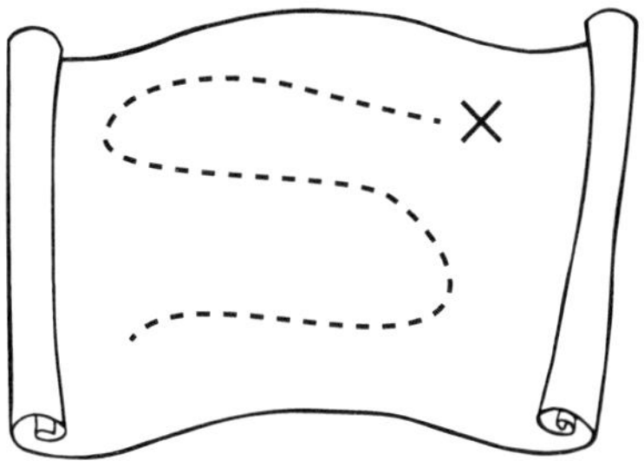

fan

rat

Colour the rat. blue
Colour the fan. red
Colour the map. green

Short a Sound

Say the name of the object out loud.
Draw a line to match the object to its word.

cab

jam

cap

Colour the jam. brown

Colour the cab. yellow

Colour the cap. purple

Short a Sound

Read the sentence to practice the words.

The rat is blue.

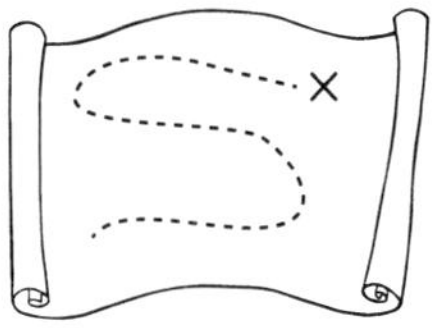

The map is green.

The fan is red.

The jam is brown.

The cap is purple.

The cab is yellow.

Colour the rat.	blue	Colour the jam.	brown
Colour the map.	green	Colour the cap.	purple
Colour the fan.	red	Colour the cab.	yellow

Short e Sound

Say the name of the object out loud.
Fill in the missing vowel for each of the words.

ĕ

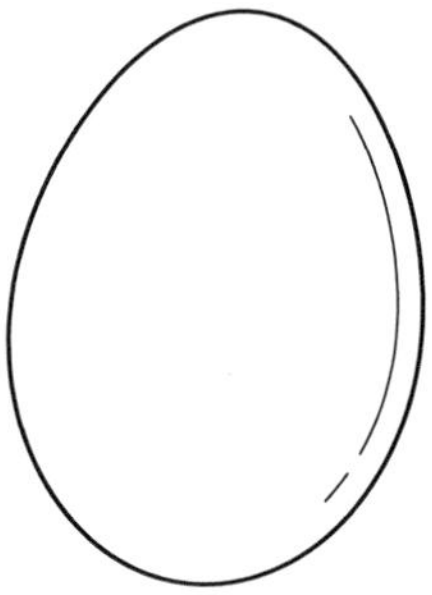

_ gg

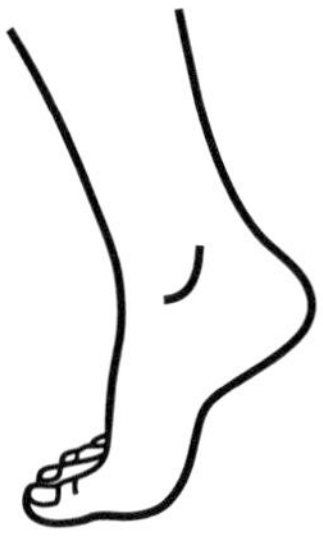

l _ g

h _ n

n _ t

w _ ll

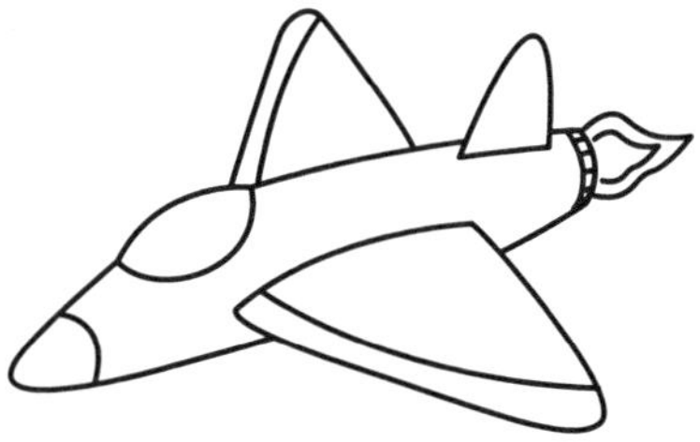

j _ t

Colour the egg.	yellow	Colour the net.	brown
Colour the leg.	green	Colour the well.	blue
Colour the hen.	red	Colour the jet.	purple

Short e Sound

Say the name of the object out loud.
Draw a line to match the object to its word.

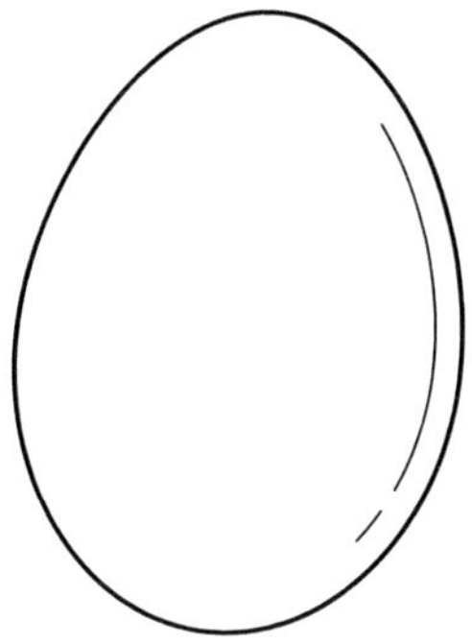

hen

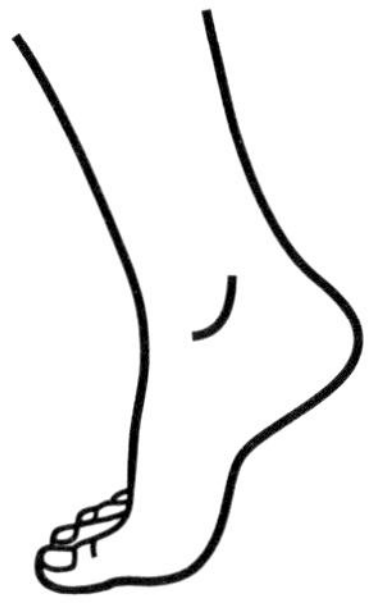

egg

leg

Colour the egg. yellow

Colour the hen. red

Colour the leg. green

Short e Sound

Say the name of the object out loud.
Draw a line to match the object to its word.

well

jet

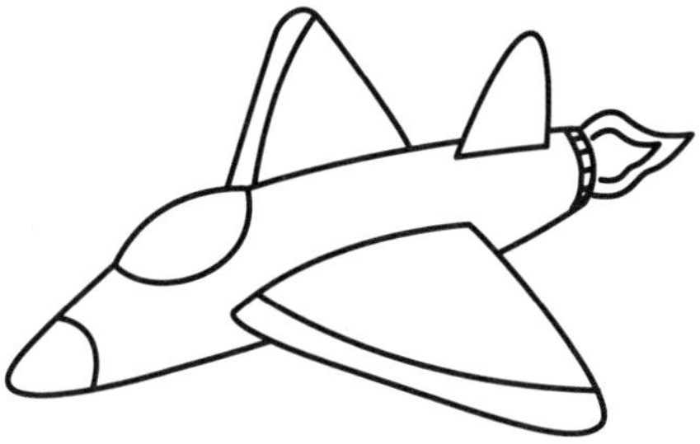

net

Colour the net. brown
Colour the jet. purple
Colour the well. blue

Short e Sound

Read the sentence to practice the words.

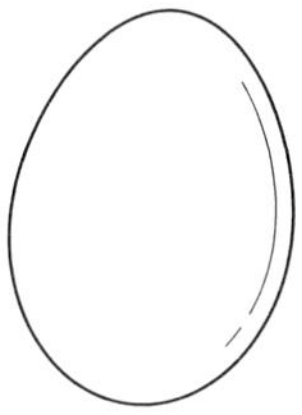

The egg is yellow.

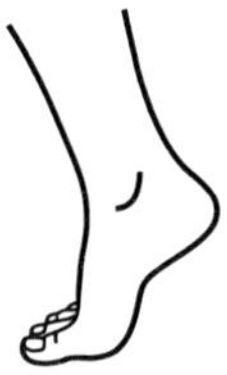

The leg is green.

The hen is red.

The net is brown.

The well is blue.

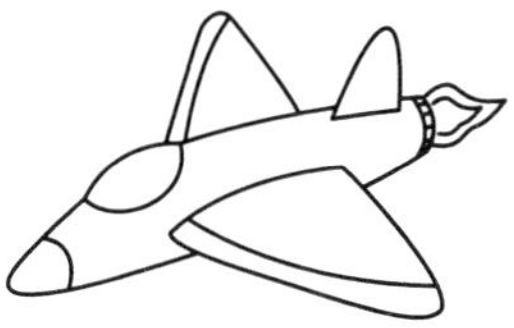

The jet is purple.

Colour the egg. 

Colour the leg. 

Colour the hen. 

Colour the net. 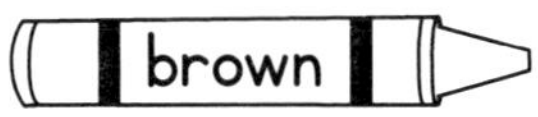

Colour the well. 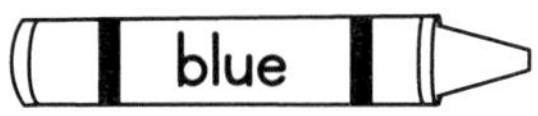

Colour the jet. 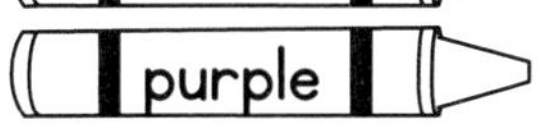

Short i Sound

Say the name of the object out loud.
Fill in the missing vowel for each of the words.

ĭ

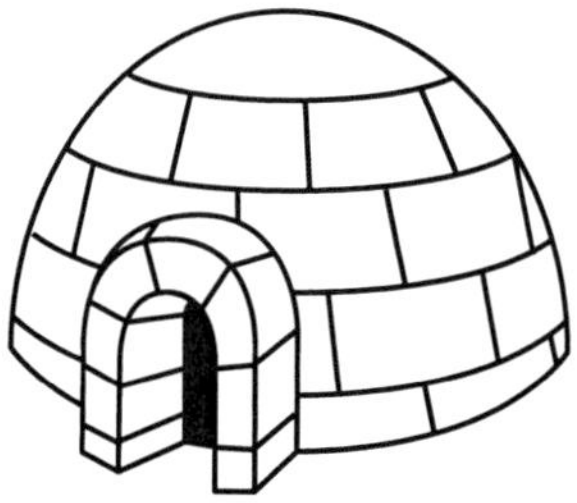

k d | gloo | f sh

f n | m lk | p g

Colour the kid.	blue	Colour the fin.	green
Colour the igloo.	yellow	Colour the milk.	purple
Colour the fish.	red	Colour the pig.	orange

Short i Sound

Say the name of the object out loud.
Draw a line to match the object to its word.

igloo

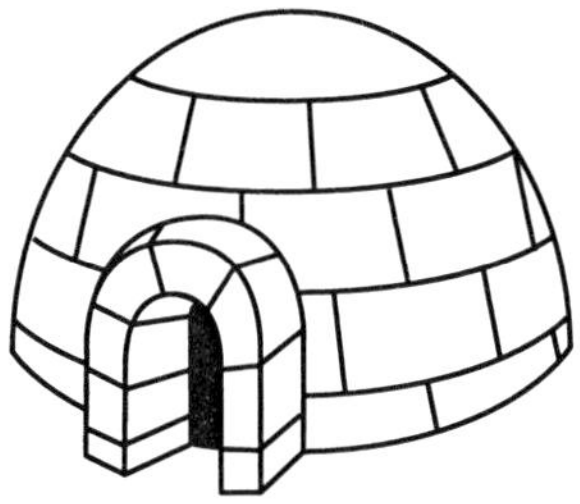

fish

kid

Colour the kid. blue
Colour the fish. red
Colour the igloo. yellow

Short i Sound

Say the name of the object out loud.
Draw a line to match the object to its word.

milk

pig

fin

Colour the fin. 

Colour the pig. 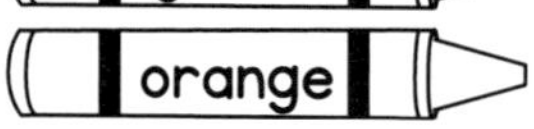

Colour the milk. 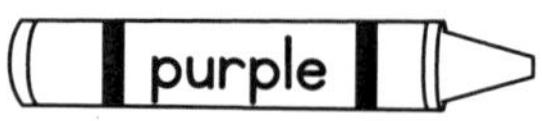

Short i Sound

Read the sentence to practice the words.

The kid is blue.

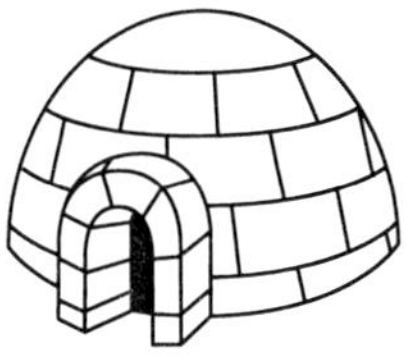

The igloo is yellow.

The fish is red.

The fin is green.

The milk is purple.

The pig is orange.

Colour the kid.	blue	Colour the fin.	green
Colour the igloo.	yellow	Colour the milk.	purple
Colour the fish.	red	Colour the pig.	orange

Short o Sound

Say the name of the object out loud.
Fill in the missing vowel for each of the words.

ŏ

l __ g   p __ t   fr __ g

d __ ll   m __ p   b __ x

Colour the log.	brown	Colour the doll.	orange
Colour the pot.	red	Colour the mop.	blue
Colour the frog.	green	Colour the box.	yellow

Short o Sound

Say the name of the object out loud.
Draw a line to match the object to its word.

frog

log

pot

Colour the log. brown
Colour the frog. green
Colour the pot. red

Short o Sound

Say the name of the object out loud.
Draw a line to match the object to its word.

mop

box

doll

Colour the doll. orange
Colour the box. yellow
Colour the mop. blue

Short o Sound

Read the sentence to practice the words.

The log is brown.

The pot is red.

The frog is green.

The doll is orange.

The mop is blue.

The box is yellow.

Colour the log.	brown	Colour the doll.	orange
Colour the pot.	red	Colour the mop.	blue
Colour the frog.	green	Colour the box.	yellow

Short u Sound

Say the name of the object out loud.
Fill in the missing vowel for each of the words.

ŭ

t b

j g

n t

b g

c p

b s

Colour the tub.	blue	Colour the bug.	red
Colour the jug.	orange	Colour the cup.	green
Colour the nut.	brown	Colour the bus.	yellow

Short u Sound

Say the name of the object out loud.
Draw a line to match the object to its word.

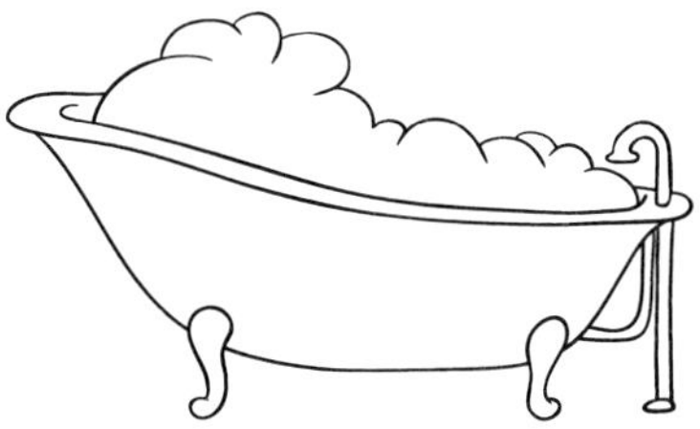

nut

tub

jug

Colour the tub. blue

Colour the nut. brown

Colour the jug. orange

Short u Sound

Say the name of the object out loud.
Draw a line to match the object to its word.

bus

bug

cup

Colour the bug. red
Colour the bus. yellow
Colour the cup. green

Short u Sound

Read the sentence to practice the words.

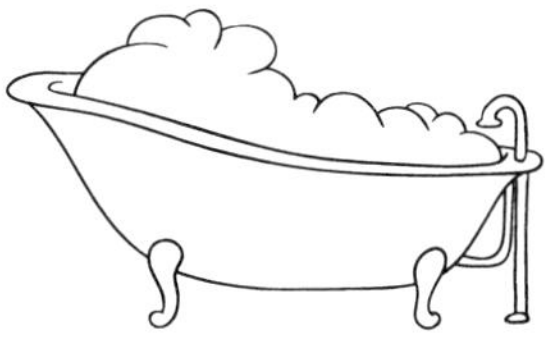

The tub is blue.

The jug is orange.

The nut is brown.

The bug is red.

The cup is green.

The bus is yellow.

Colour the tub.	blue	Colour the bug.	red
Colour the jug.	orange	Colour the cup.	green
Colour the nut.	brown	Colour the bus.	yellow

Long a Sound

Say the name of the object out loud.
Fill in the missing vowel for each of the words.

ā

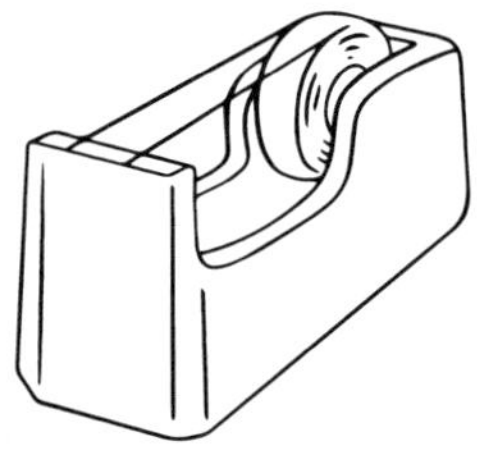

t ___ pe

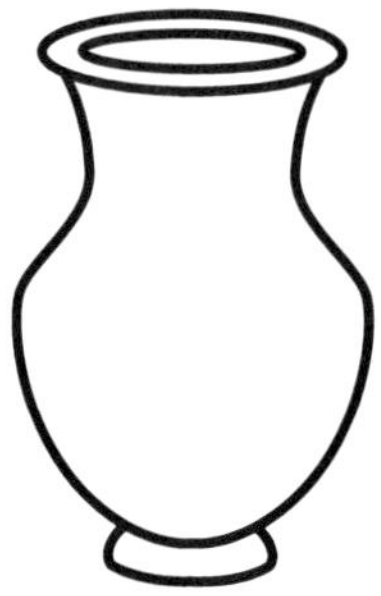

v ___ se

___ pe

r ___ ke

g ___ me

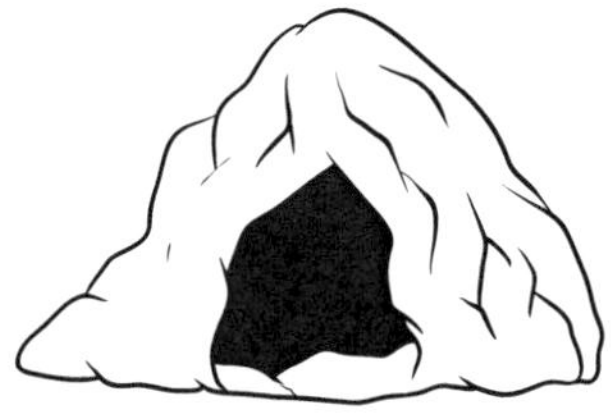

c ___ ve

Colour the tape.	red	Colour the rake.	red
Colour the vase.	green	Colour the game.	purple
Colour the ape.	brown	Colour the cave.	orange

Long a Sound

Say the name of the object out loud.
Draw a line to match the object to its word.

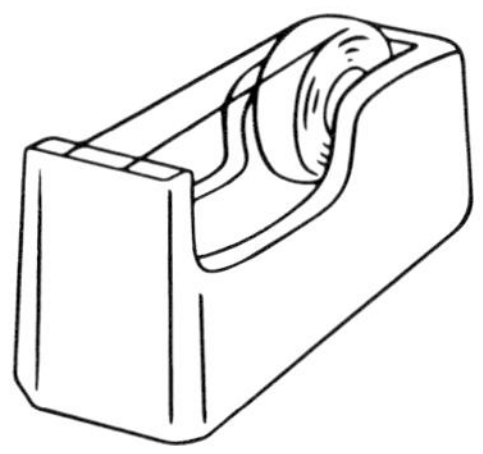

ape

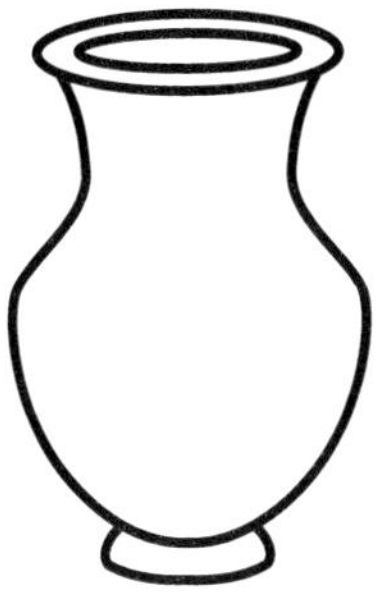

tape

vase

Colour the tape. red
Colour the ape. brown
Colour the vase. green

Long a Sound

Say the name of the object out loud.
Draw a line to match the object to its word.

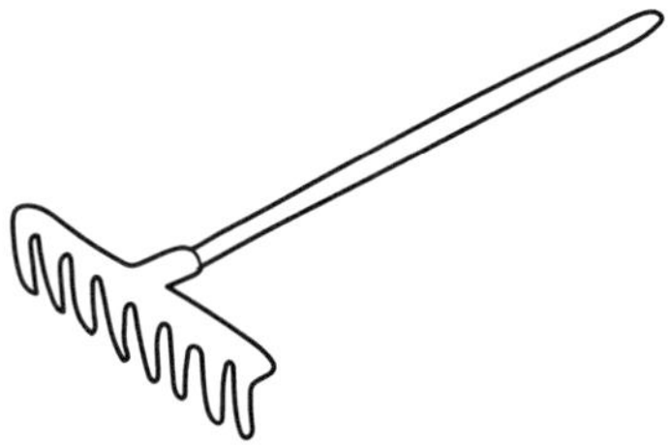

cave

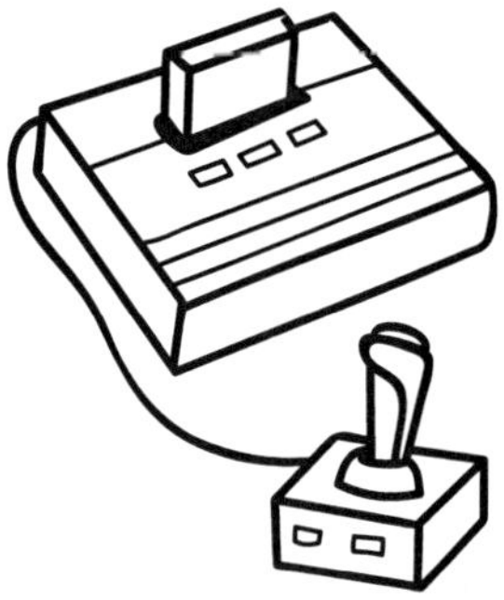

rake

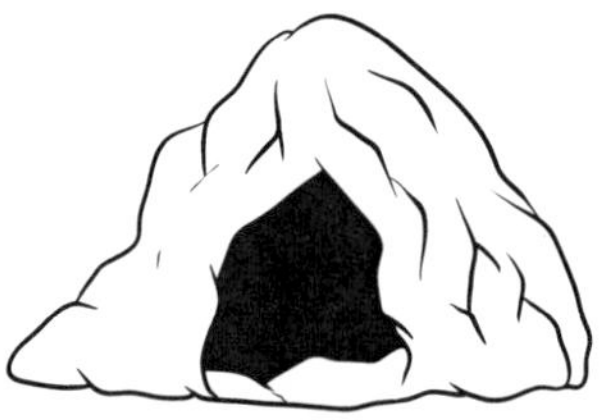

game

Colour the rake. red
Colour the cave. orange
Colour the game. purple

Long a Sound

Read the sentence to practice the words.

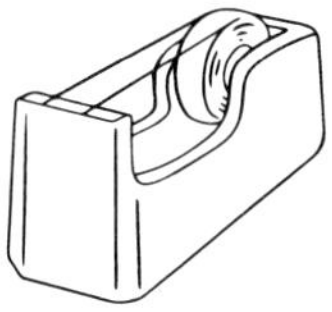

The tape is red.

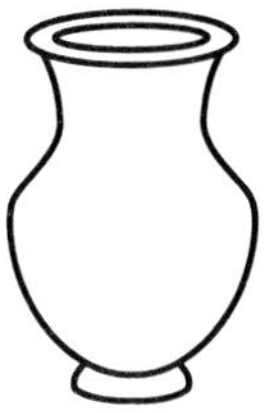

The vase is green.

The ape is brown.

The rake is red.

The game is purple.

The cave is orange.

Colour the tape.	red	Colour the rake.	red
Colour the vase.	green	Colour the game.	purple
Colour the ape.	brown	Colour the cave.	orange

Long e Sound

Say the name of the object out loud.
Fill in the missing vowel for each of the words.

ē

b e

tr e

s al

j ep

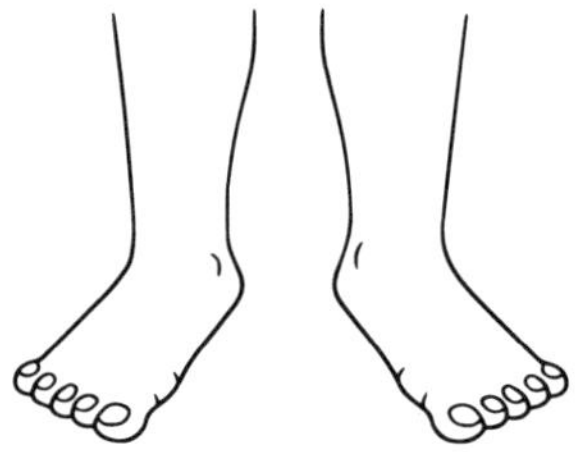

f et

b ak

Colour the bee. yellow
Colour the tree. green
Colour the seal. blue
Colour the jeep. brown
Colour the feet. purple
Colour the beak. orange

Long e Sound

Say the name of the object out loud.
Draw a line to match the object to its word.

beak

seal

bee

Colour the bee. yellow
Colour the seal. blue
Colour the beak. green

Long e Sound

Say the name of the object out loud.
Draw a line to match the object to its word.

tree

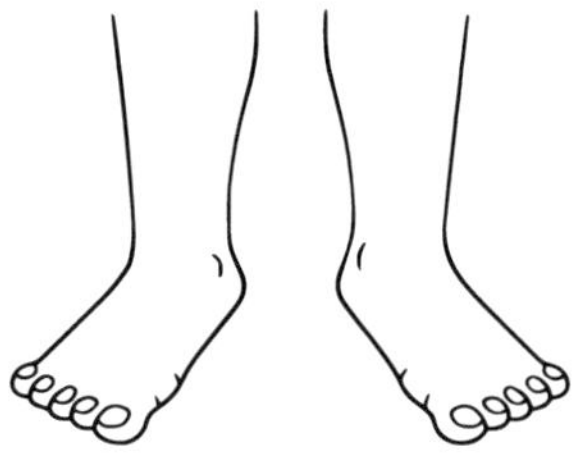

jeep

feet

Colour the jeep. brown
Colour the tree. orange
Colour the feet. purple

Long e Sound

Read the sentence to practice the words.

The bee is yellow.

The tree is green.

The seal is blue.

The jeep is brown.

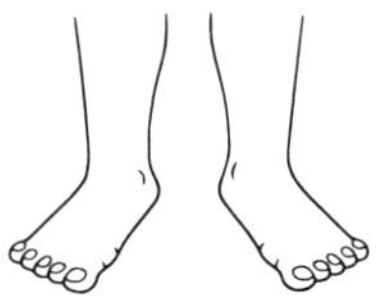

The feet are purple.

The beak is orange.

Colour the bee.	yellow	Colour the jeep.	brown
Colour the tree.	green	Colour the feet.	purple
Colour the seal.	blue	Colour the beak.	orange

Long i Sound

Say the name of the object out loud.
Fill in the missing vowel for each of the words.

ī

sl _ de

v _ ne

t _ re

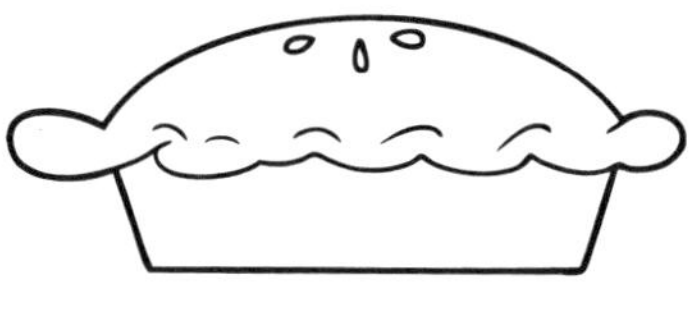

p _ e

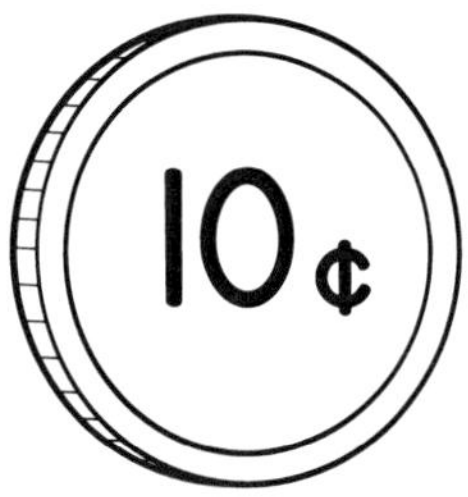

d _ me

h _ ve

Colour the slide.	red	Colour the pie.	brown
Colour the vine.	green	Colour the dime.	yellow
Colour the tire.	blue	Colour the hive.	orange

Long i Sound

Say the name of the object out loud.
Draw a line to match the object to its word.

tire

slide

vine

Colour the slide. red
Colour the tire. blue
Colour the vine. green

Long i Sound

Say the name of the object out loud.
Draw a line to match the object to its word.

dime

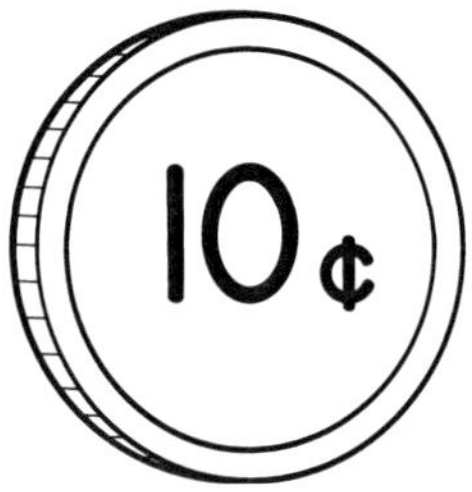

hive

pie

Colour the pie. brown
Colour the hive. orange
Colour the dime. yellow

Long i Sound

Read the sentence to practice the words.

The slide is red.

The vine is green.

The tire is blue.

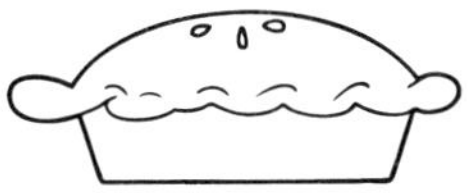

The pie is brown.

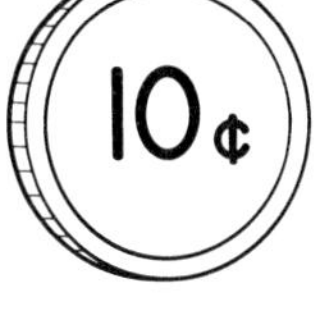

The dime is yellow.

The hive is orange.

Colour the slide.	red	Colour the pie.	brown
Colour the vine.	green	Colour the dime.	yellow
Colour the tire.	blue	Colour the hive.	orange

Long o Sound

Say the name of the object out loud.
Fill in the missing vowel for each of the words.

ō

n te

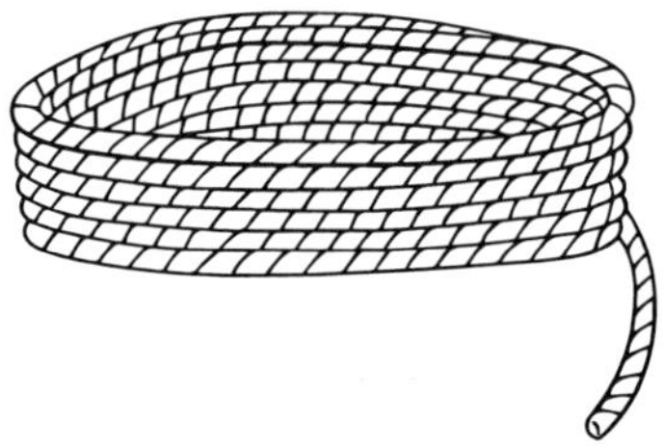

r pe

ph ne

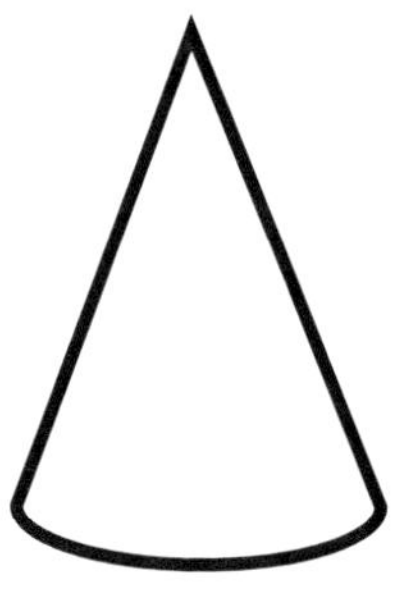

c ne

p le

r se

Colour the note.	red	Colour the cone.	brown
Colour the rope.	yellow	Colour the pole.	purple
Colour the phone.	blue	Colour the rose.	orange

Long o Sound

Say the name of the object out loud.
Draw a line to match the object to its word.

rope

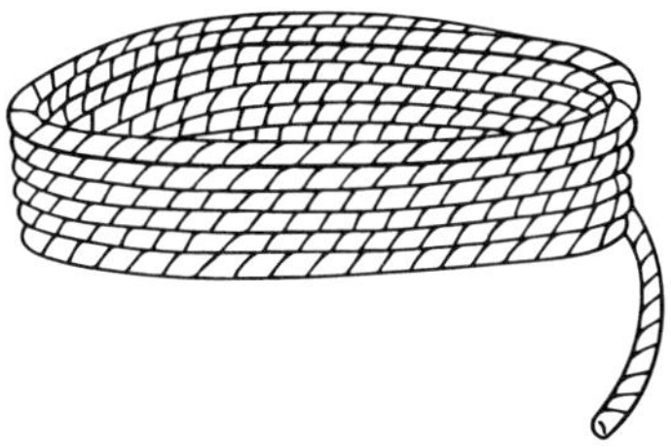

phone

note

Colour the note. red
Colour the phone. blue
Colour the rope. yellow

Long o Sound

Say the name of the object out loud.
Draw a line to match the object to its word.

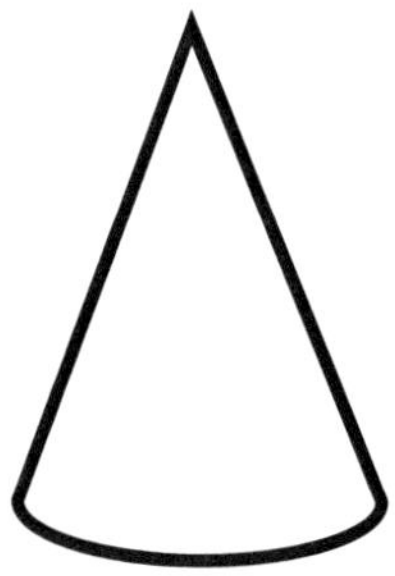

pole

rose

cone

Colour the cone. brown
Colour the rose. orange
Colour the pole. purple

Long o Sound

Read the sentence to practice the words.

The note is red.

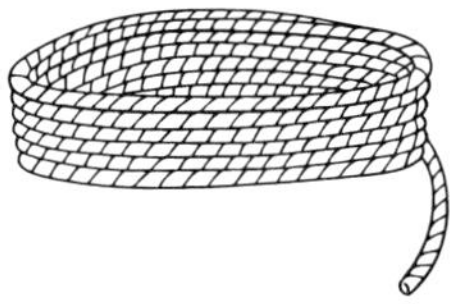

The rope is yellow.

The phone is blue.

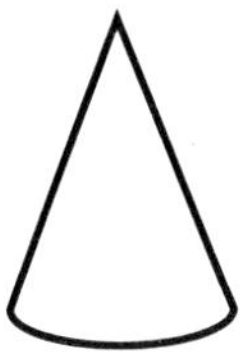

The cone is brown.

The pole is purple.

The rose is orange.

Colour the note. red

Colour the rope. yellow

Colour the phone. blue

Colour the cone. brown

Colour the pole. purple

Colour the rose. orange

Long u Sound

Say the name of the object out loud.
Fill in the missing vowel for each of the words.

ū

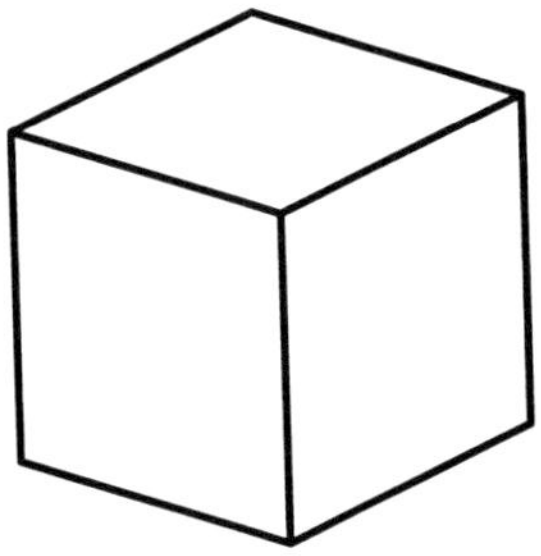

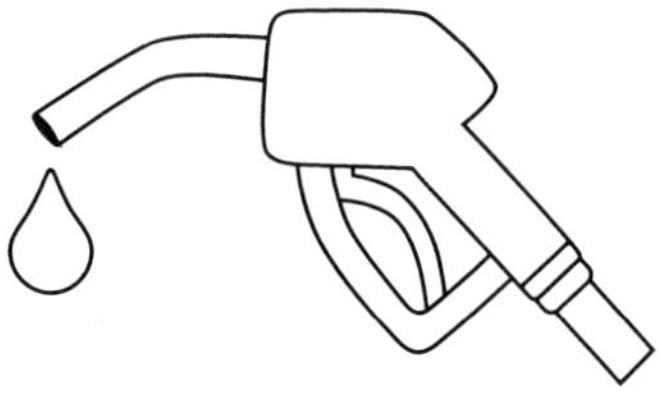

c ___ be   f ___ el   J ___ ne

m ___ le   men ___   arg ___ e

Colour the cube. red
Colour the fuel. yellow
Colour the June. blue
Colour the mule. brown
Colour the menu. purple
Colour argue. orange

Long u Sound

Say the name of the object out loud.
Draw a line to match the object to its word.

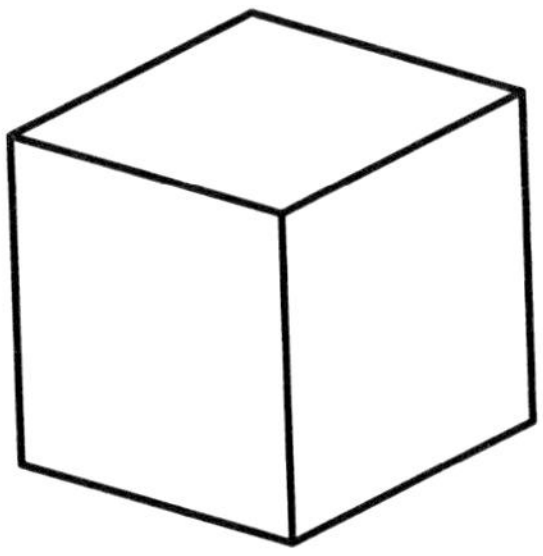

fuel

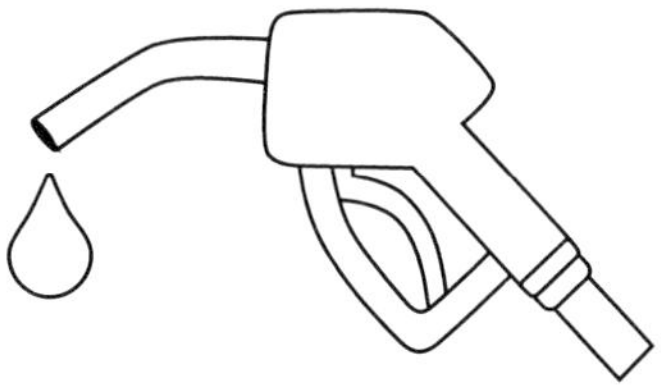

June

cube

Colour the cube. red

Colour the June. blue

Colour the fuel. yellow

Long u Sound

Say the name of the object out loud.
Draw a line to match the object to its word.

argue

mule

menu

Colour the mule. brown
Colour argue. orange
Colour the menu. purple

Long u Sound

Read the sentence to practice the words.

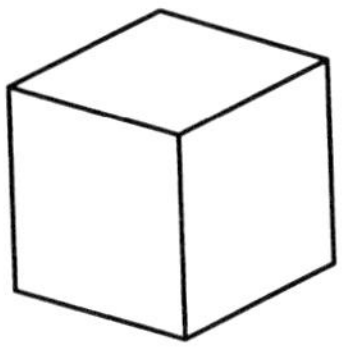

The cube is red.

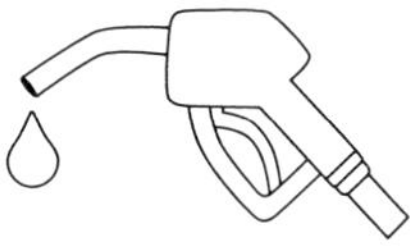

The fuel is yellow.

The June is blue.

The mule is brown.

The menu is purple.

Argue is orange.

Colour the cube. red
Colour the fuel. yellow
Colour the June. blue

Colour the mule. brown
Colour the menu. purple
Colour argue. orange

Y as Long i Sound

Sometimes the letter y makes a long i sound.

fly

The fly is brown.

sky

The sky is orange.

cry

The cry is blue.

fry

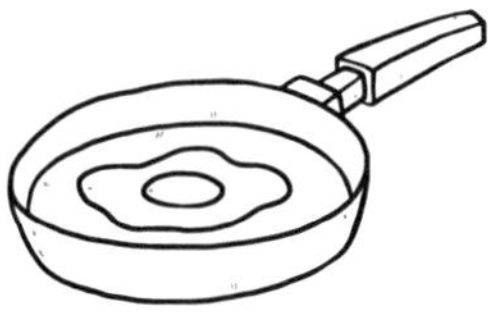

The fry is yellow.

Colour the fly. 

Colour the sky. 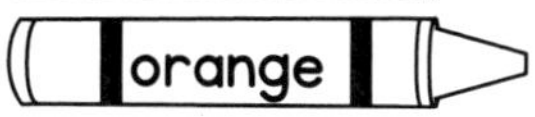

Colour the cry. 

Colour the fry. 

Y as Long e Sound

Sometimes the letter y makes a long **e** sound.

bunny

The bunny is brown.

baby

The baby is blue.

lady

The lady is green.

puppy

The puppy is orange.

Colour the bunny. brown
Colour the baby. blue
Colour the lady. green
Colour the puppy. orange

Digraphs - CH

Circle the objects that begin with 'ch'.

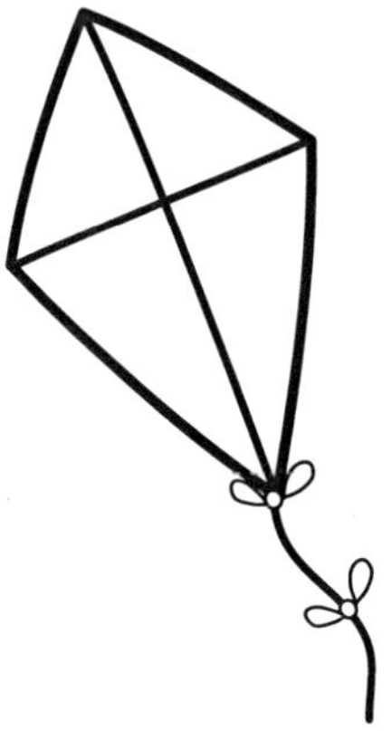

Digraphs - TH

Circle the objects that begin with 'th'.

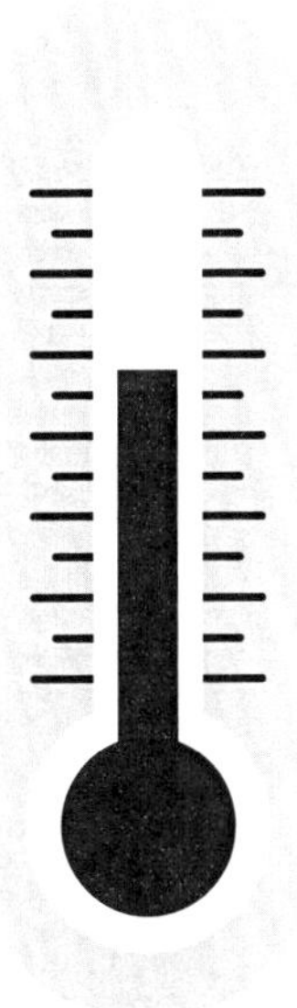

Digraphs - SH

Circle the objects that begin with 'sh'.

Digraphs - WH

Circle the objects that begin with 'wh'.

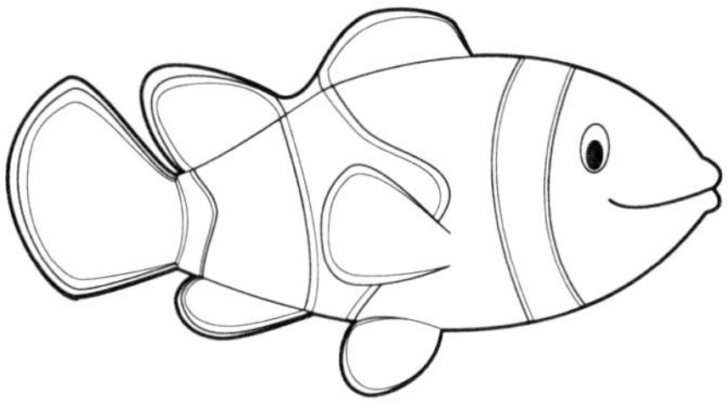

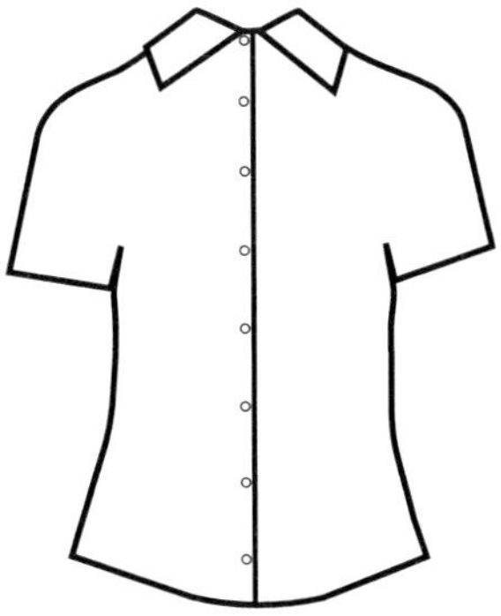

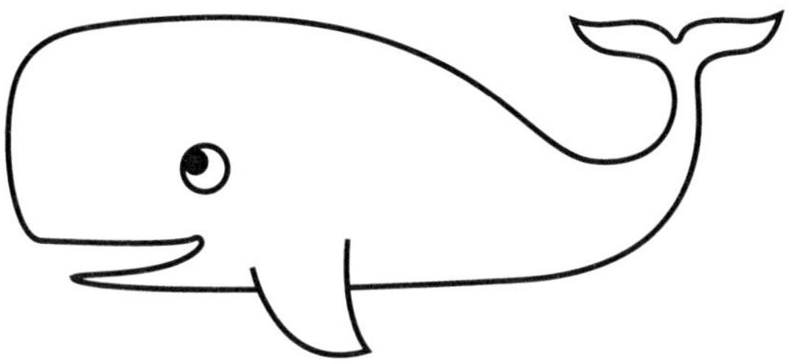

Counting Syllables

Clap the syllables as you say the word.
Circle the number of syllables.

apple

1 2 3

ladybug

1 2 3

net

1 2 3

Counting Syllables

Say the name of the object out loud.
Circle the number of syllables.

1 2 3

1 2 3

1 2 3

1 2 3

1 2 3

1 2 3

Colour the balloons. red
Colour the elephant. blue
Colour the frog. green
Colour the umbrella. orange
Colour the sun. yellow
Colour the guitar. brown

Number Skills

Number Cards

0	1	2
3	4	5
6	7	8
9	10	

Number 0

There are 0 eggs.

Trace and print.
Circle your best 0 on each line.

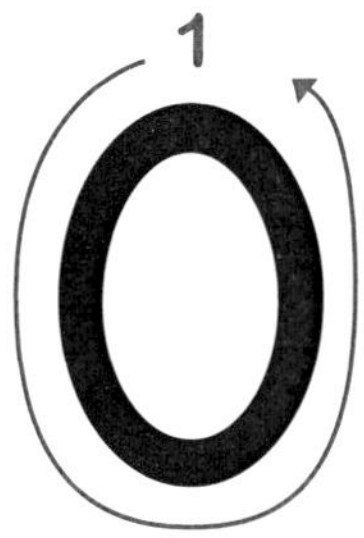

Number 0

Draw s to show the number 0.

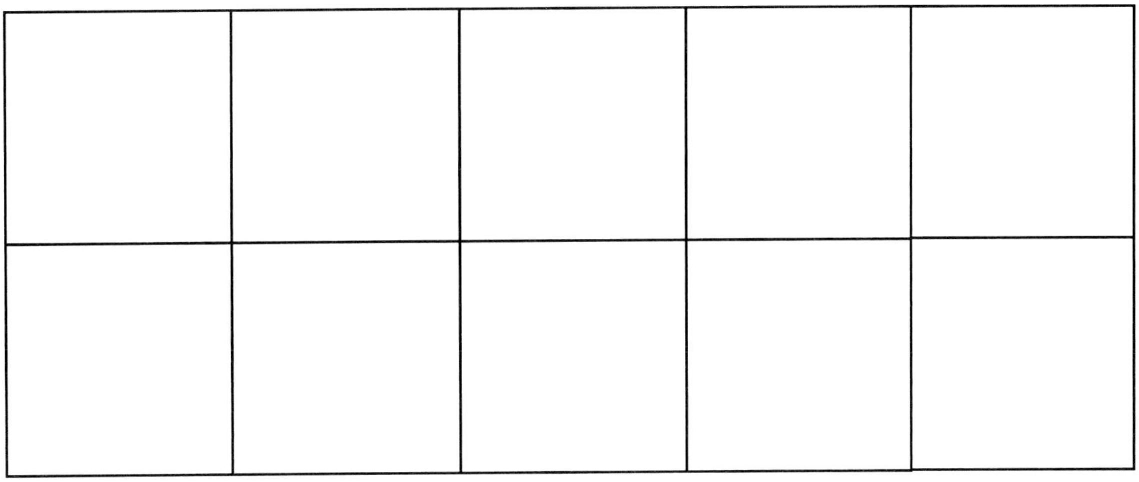

Trace and print.
Circle your best 0 on each line.

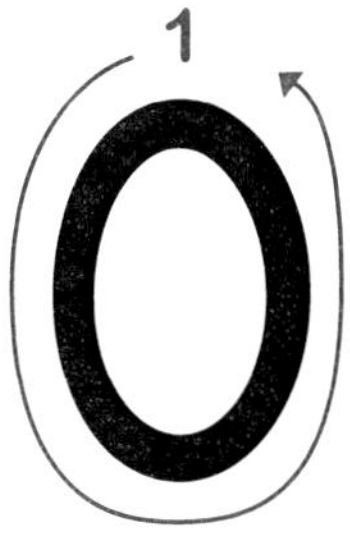

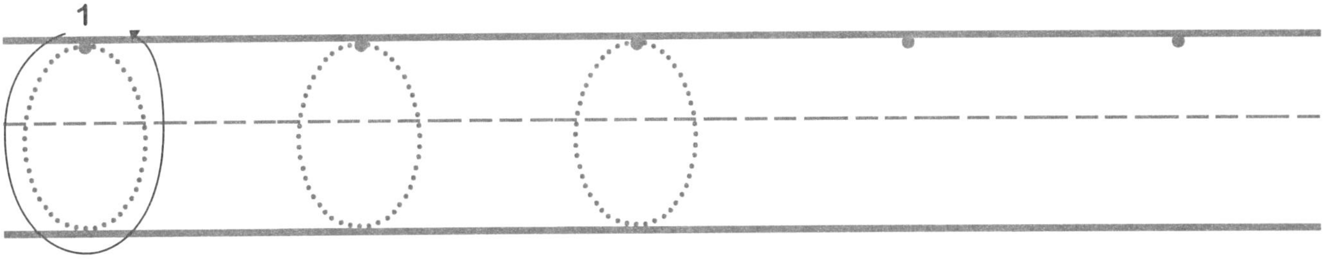

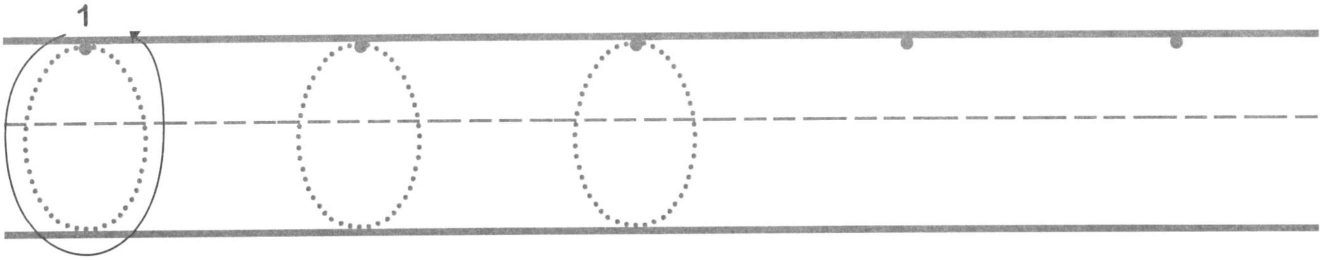

Number 1

There is 1 airplane.

Trace and print.

Circle your best 1 on each line.

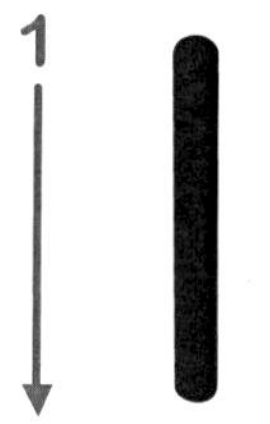

Number 1

Draw ●s to show the number 1.

Trace and print.

Circle your best 1 on each line.

Number 2

There are 2 penguins.

Trace and print.

Circle your best 2 on each line.

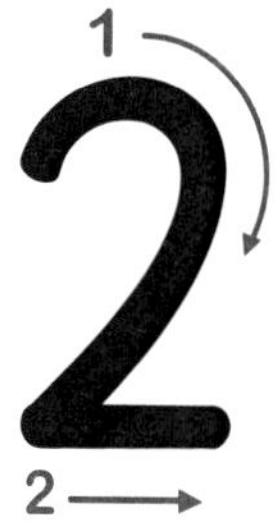

Number 2

Draw ●s to show the number 2.

Trace and print.

Circle your best 2 on each line.

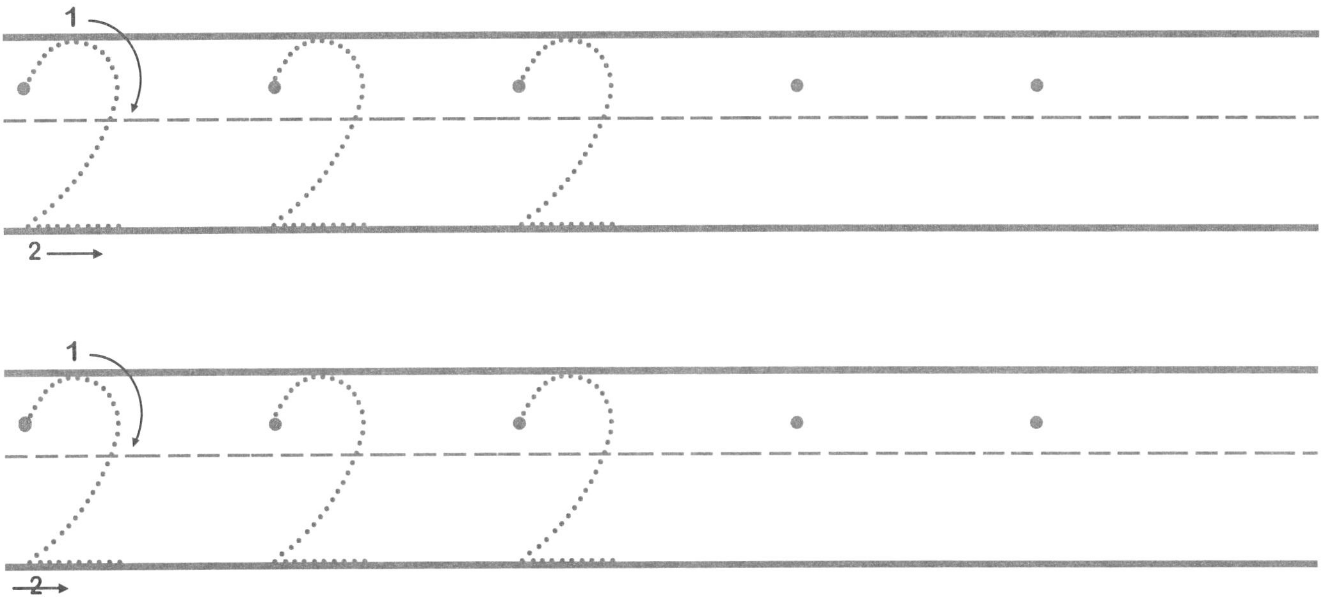

Number 3

There are 3 fish.

Trace and print.

Circle your best 3 on each line.

3

Number 3

Draw ●s to show the number 3.

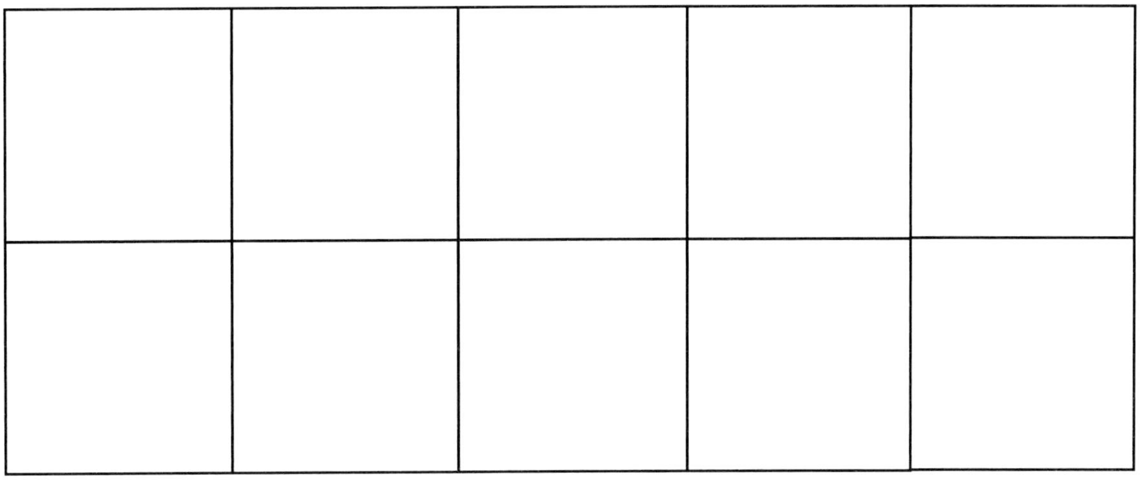

Trace and print.

Circle your best 3 on each line.

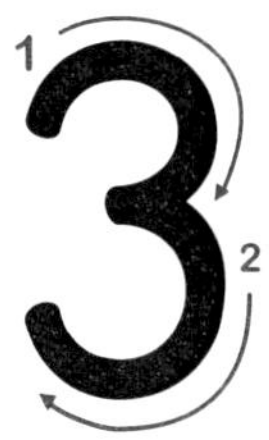

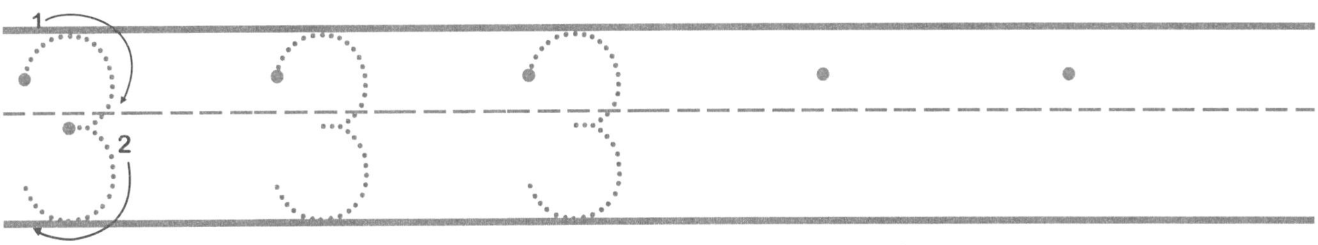

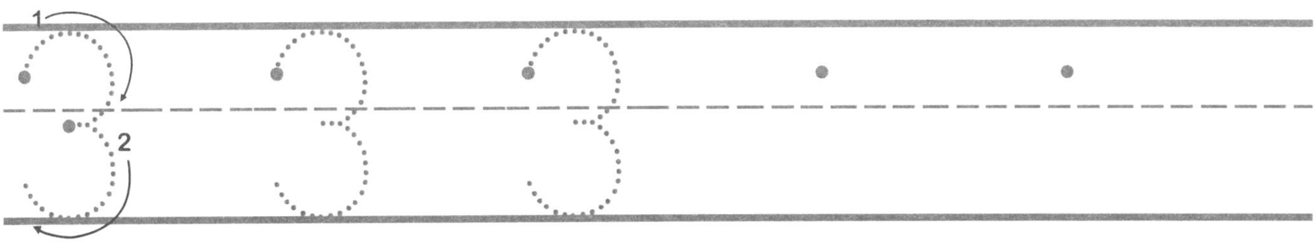

Number 4

There are 4 yo-yos.

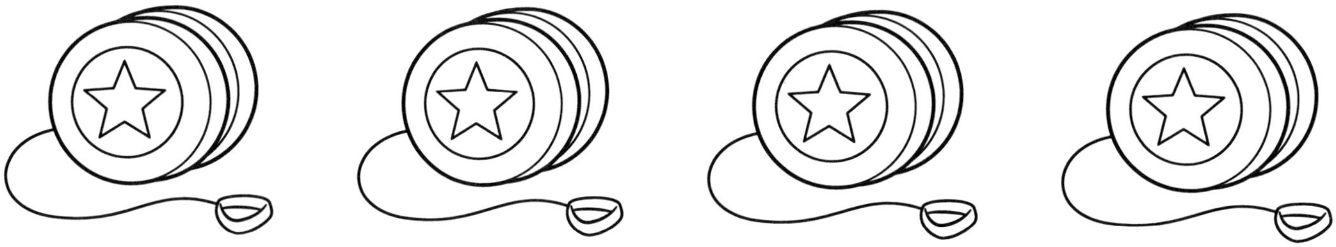

Trace and print.
Circle your best 4 on each line.

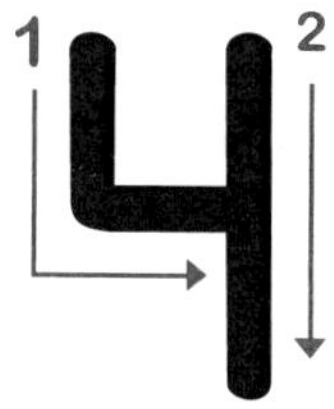

Number 4

Draw ●s to show the number 4.

Trace and print.
Circle your best 4 on each line.

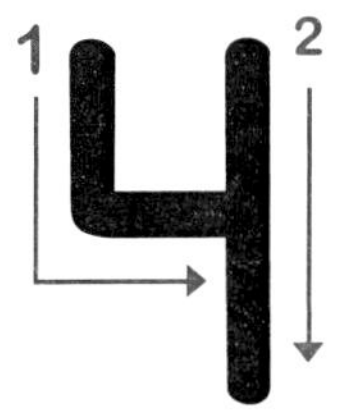

Number 5

There are 5 owls.

Trace and print.

Circle your best 5 on each line.

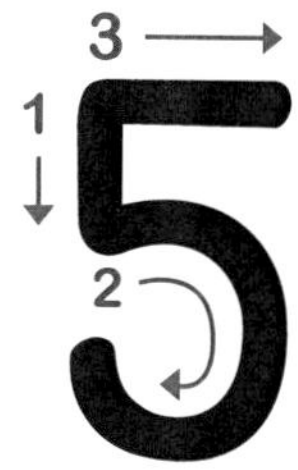

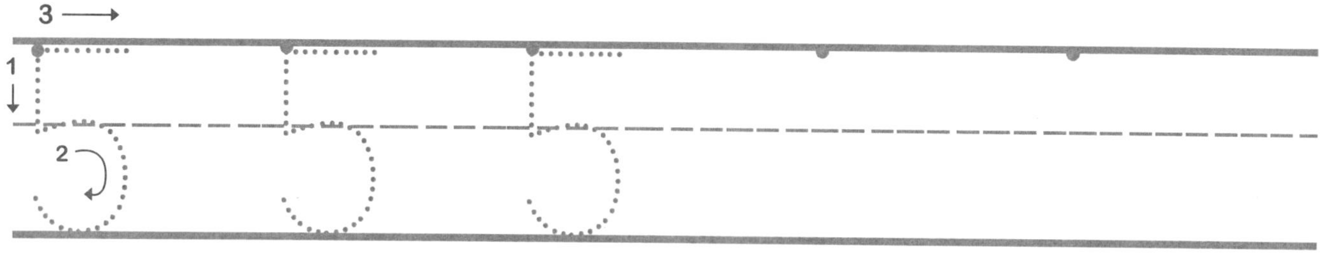

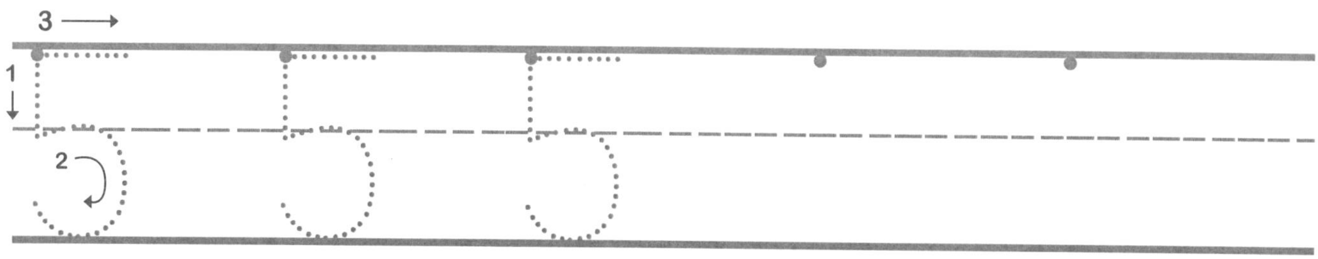

Number 5

Draw ●s to show the number 5.

Trace and print.

Circle your best 5 on each line.

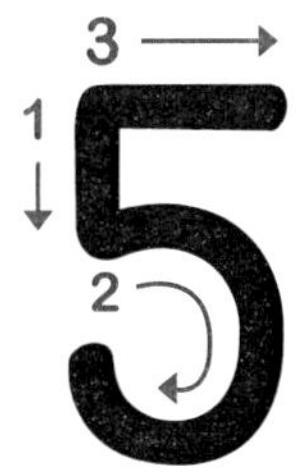

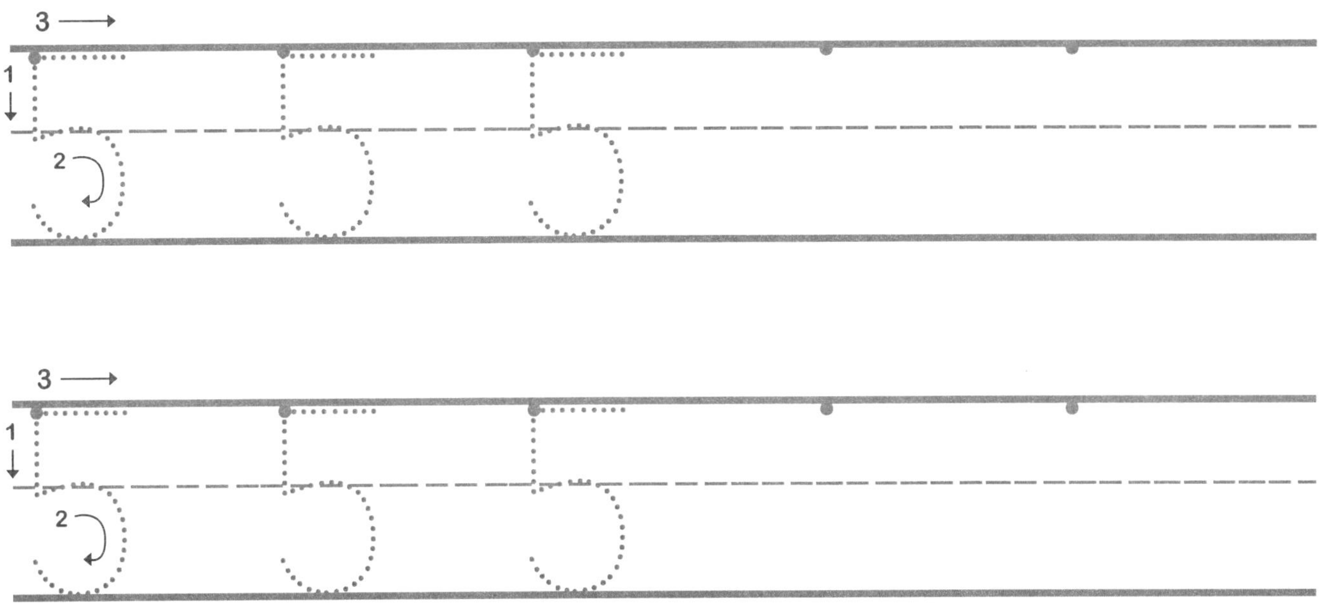

Number 6

There are 6 trees.

Trace and print.

Circle your best 6 on each line.

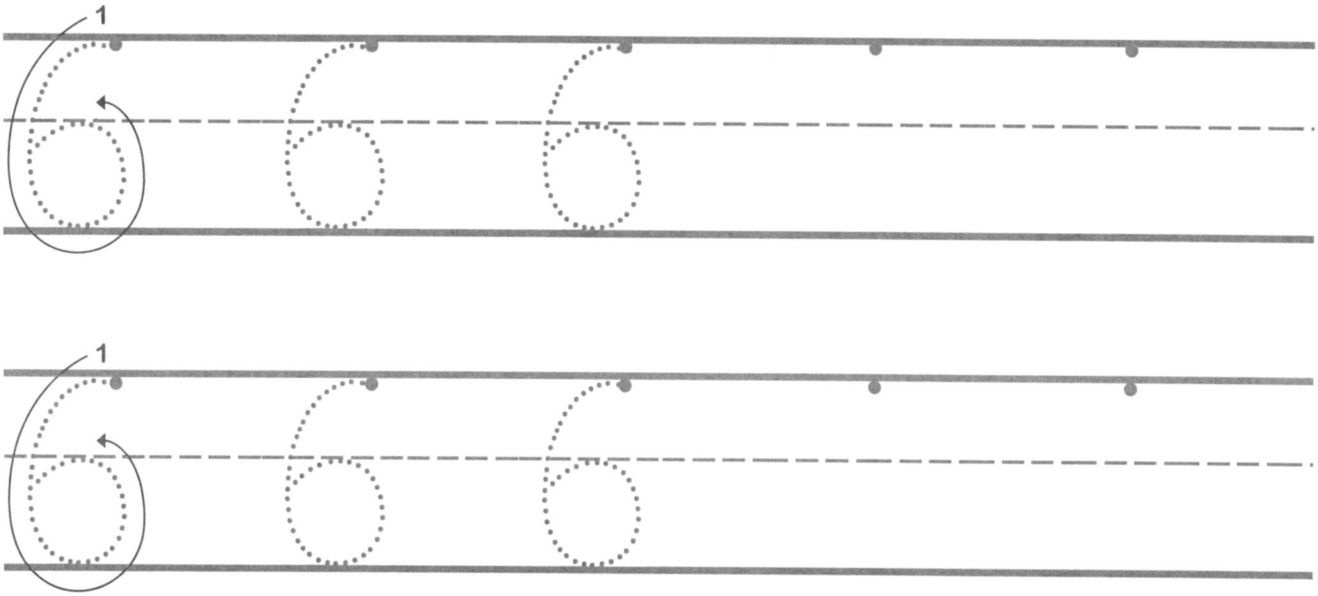

Number 6

Draw ●s to show the number 6.

Trace and print.

Circle your best 6 on each line.

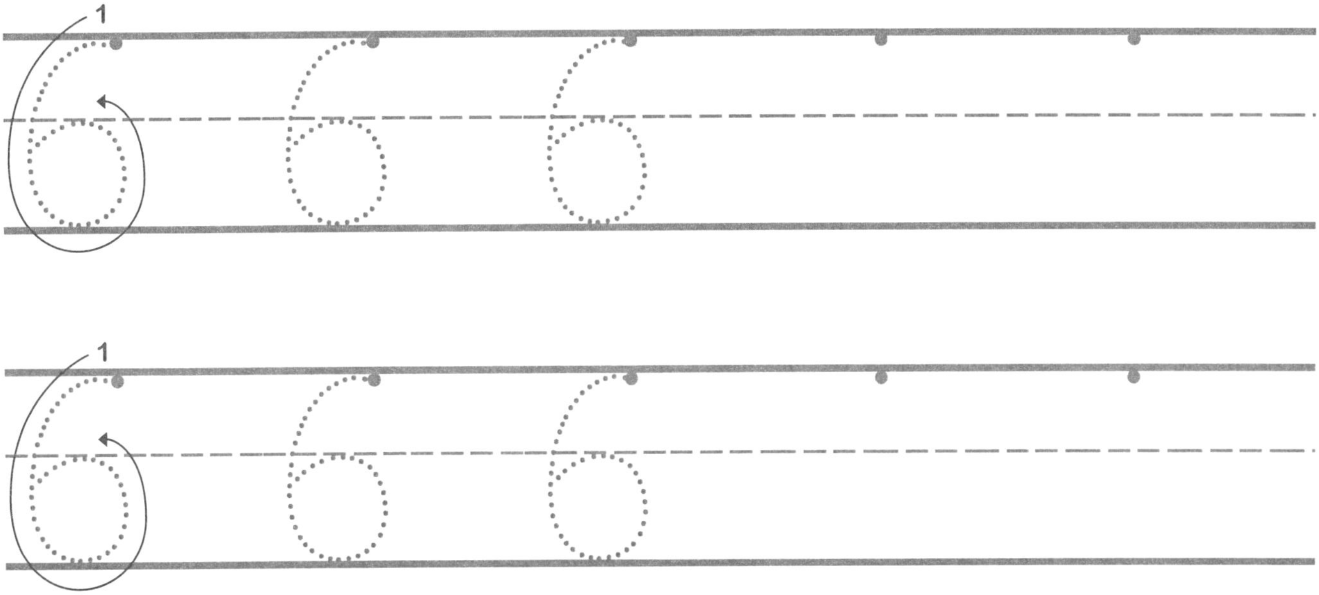

Number 7

There are 7 eagles.

Trace and print.

Circle your best 7 on each line.

7

Number 7

Draw ●s to show the number 7.

Trace and print.

Circle your best 7 on each line.

Number 8

There are 8 ladybugs.

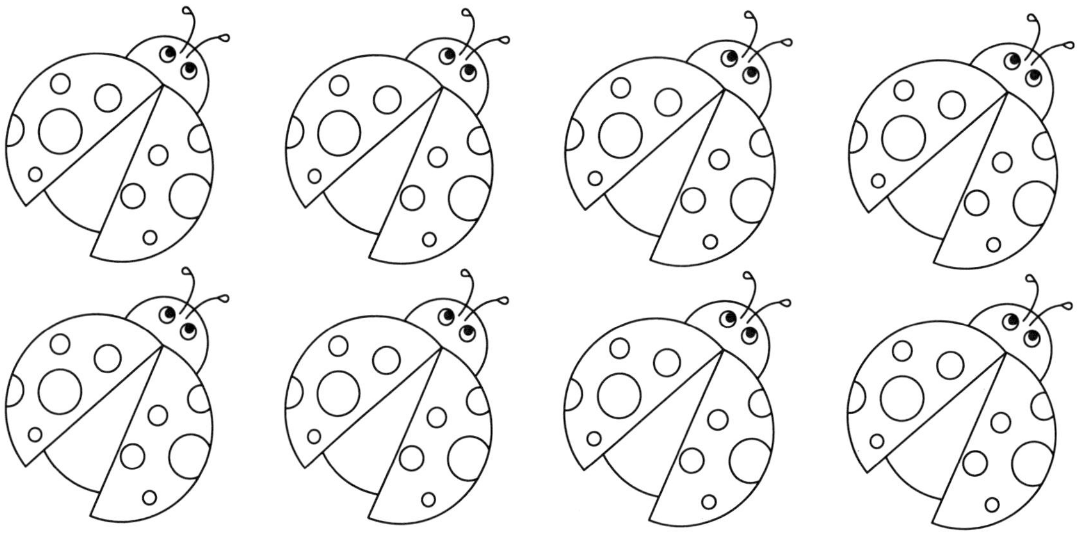

Trace and print.

Circle your best 8 on each line.

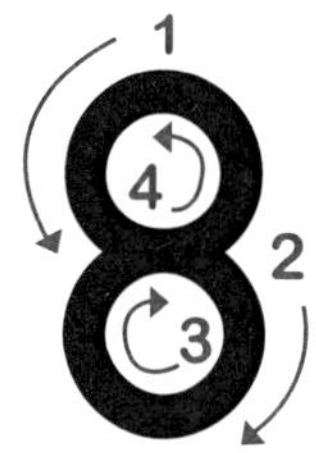

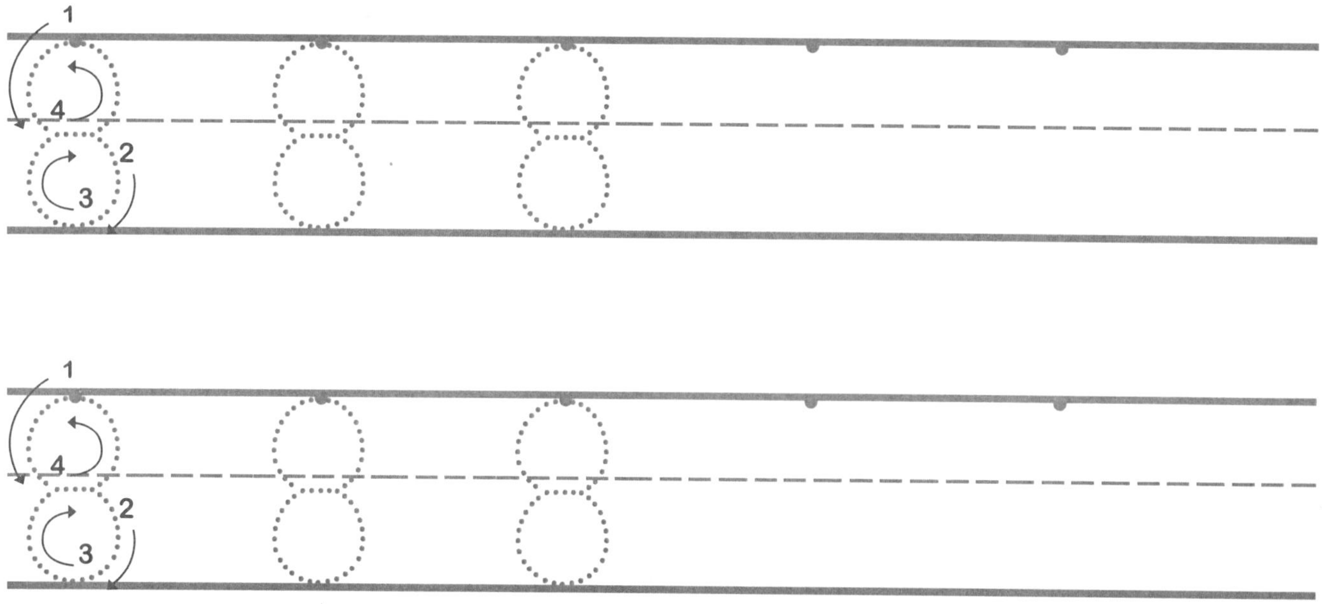

Number 8

Draw ●s to show the number 8.

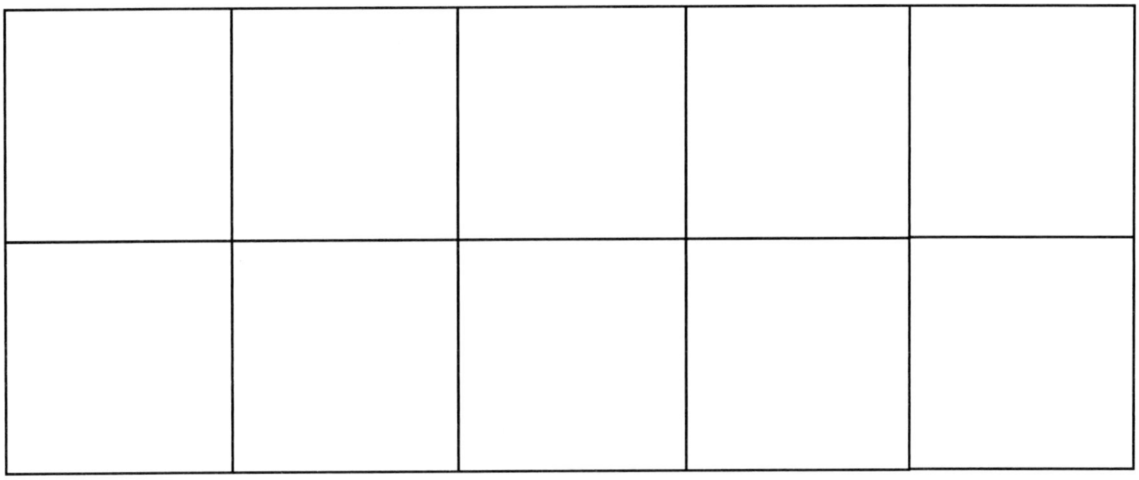

Trace and print.

Circle your best 8 on each line.

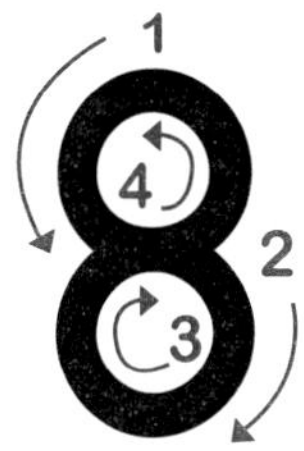

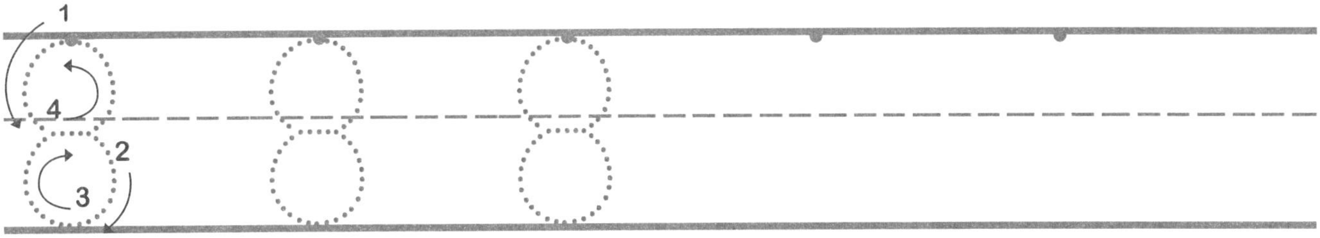

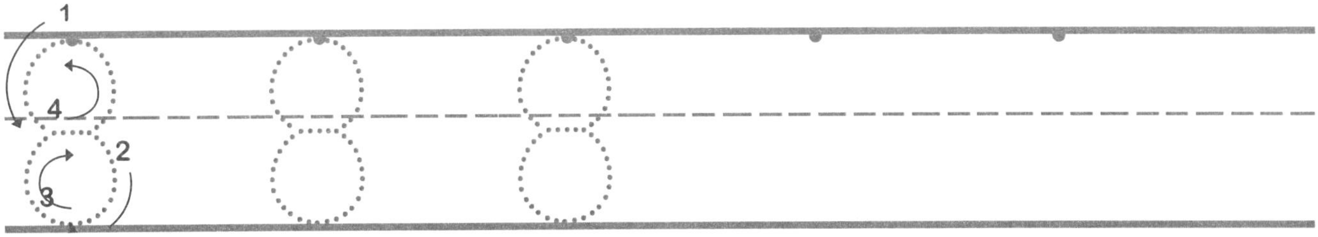

Number 9

There are 9 queens.

Trace and print.

Circle your best 9 on each line.

Number 9

Draw ●s to show the number 9.

Trace and print.

Circle your best 9 on each line.

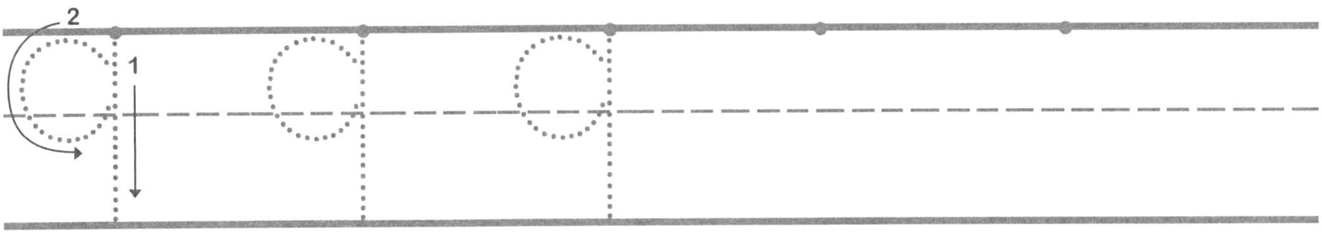

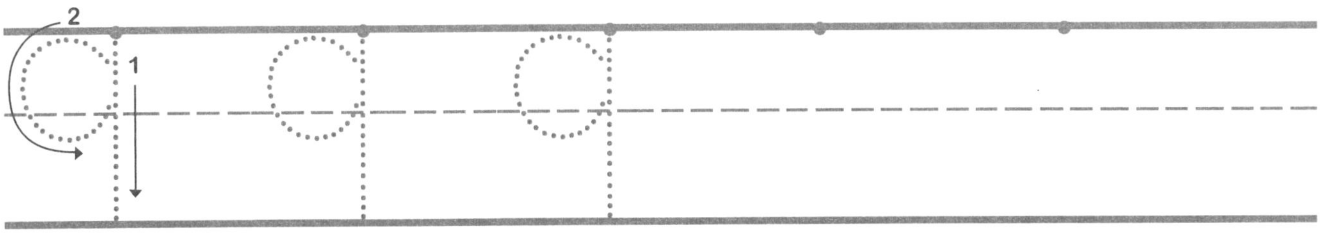

Number 10

There are 10 butterflies.

Trace and print.

Circle your best 10 on each line.

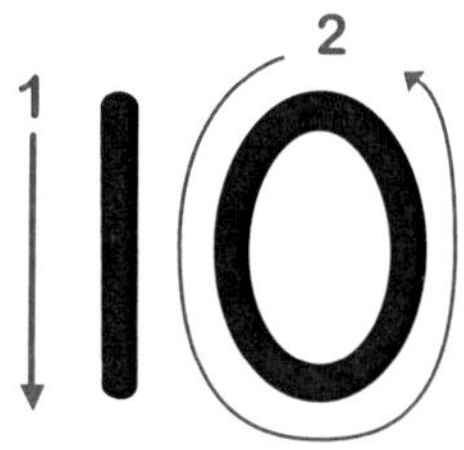

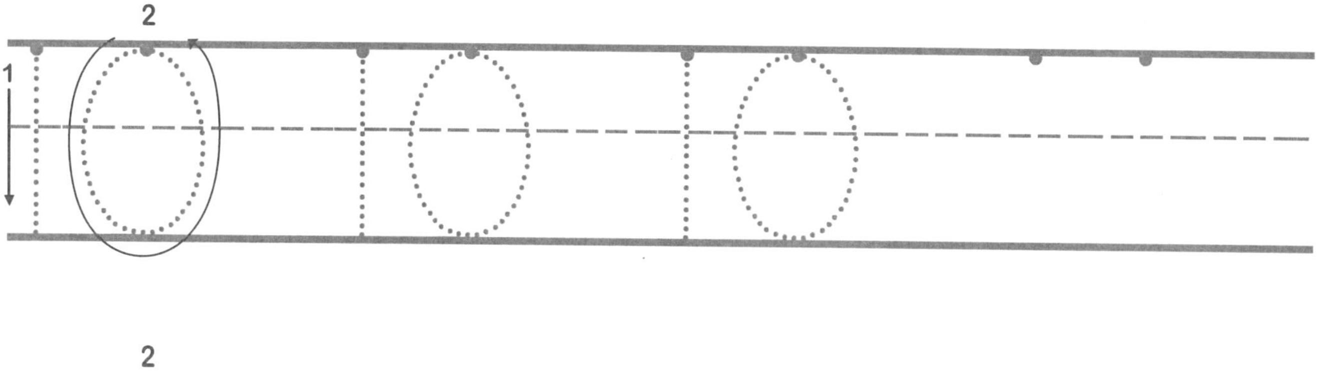

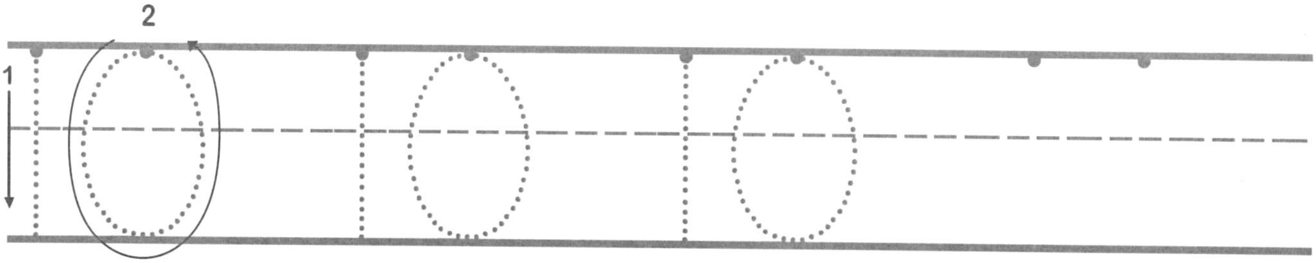

Number 10

Draw ●s to show the number 10.

Trace and print.

Circle your best 10 on each line.

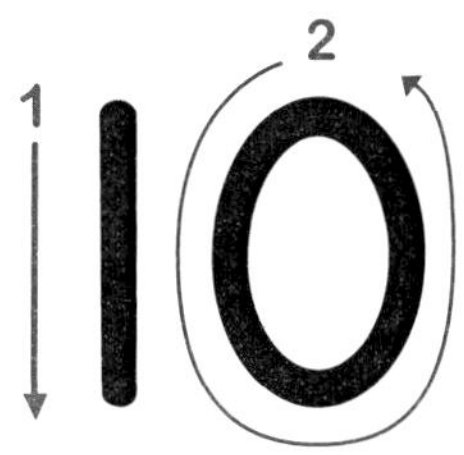

Ten Frames: 0-10

Trace the number. Draw s to show the number.

3

6

8

10

1

5

Ten Frames: 0-10

Trace the number. Draw ●s to show the number.

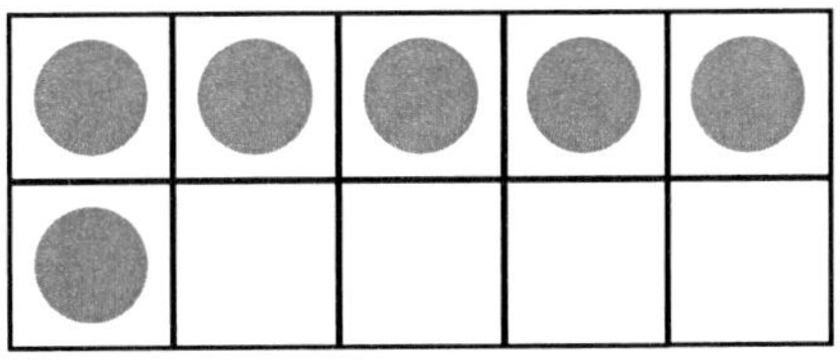

6

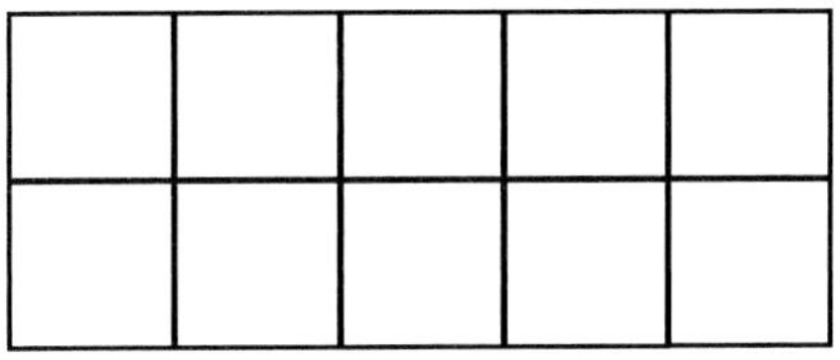

2

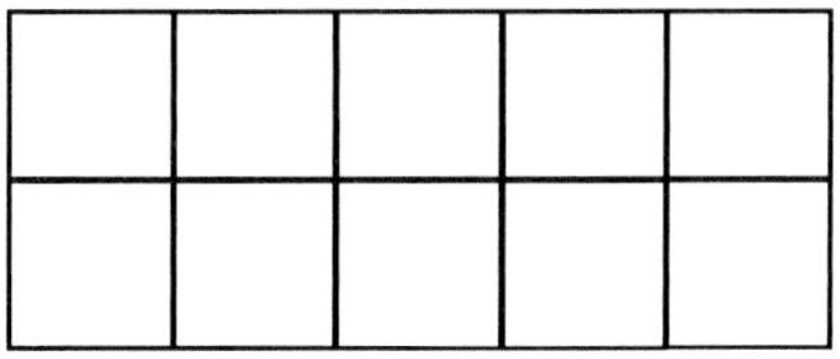

9

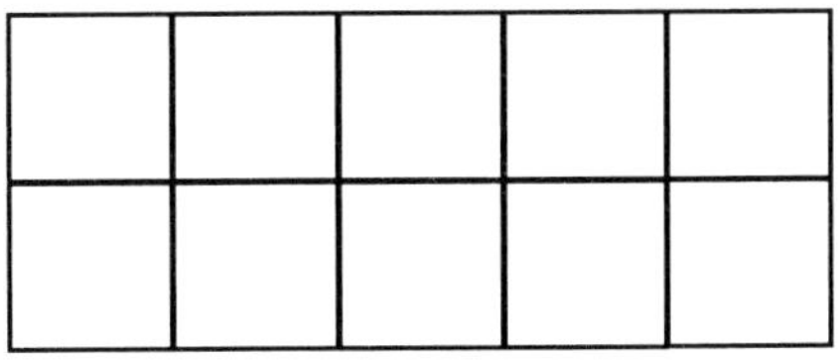

4

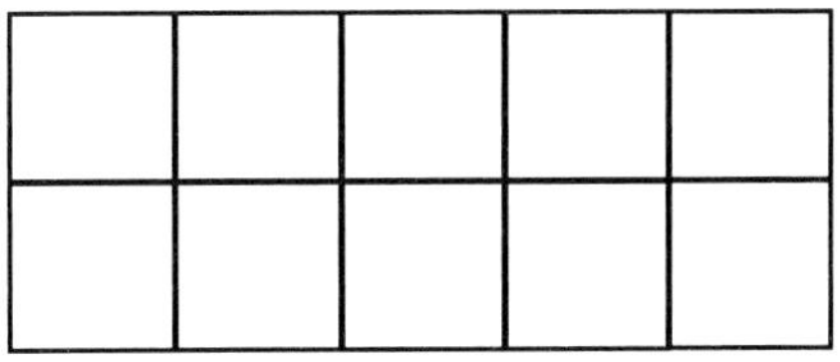

7

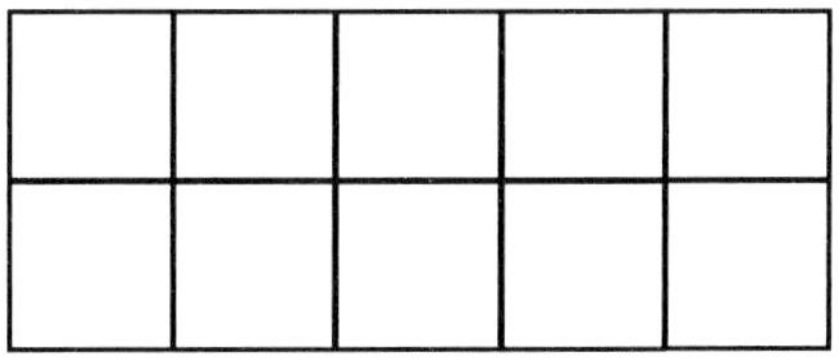

3

Colouring by Number: 0-5

Colour the object using the colour key.

Think About It!

What do you call a bear with no teeth?
A gummy bear!

0 - red
1 - orange
2 - yellow
3 - green
4 - brown
5 - black

Colouring by Number: 6-10

Colour the object using the colour key.

Think About It!

What do you call cold penguin?
A brrrrd!

6 - red
7 - orange
8 - yellow
9 - blue
10 - black

Counting with Fingers: 0-10

How many fingers are there? Circle the correct number.

1	2	3

7	8	9

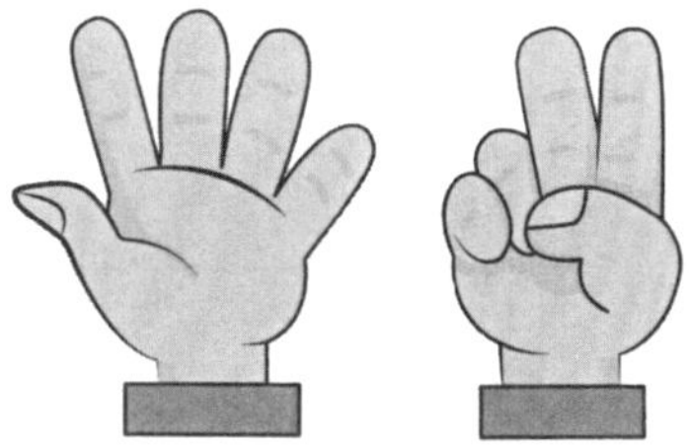

6	7	8

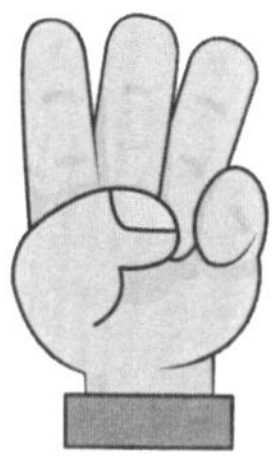

2	3	4

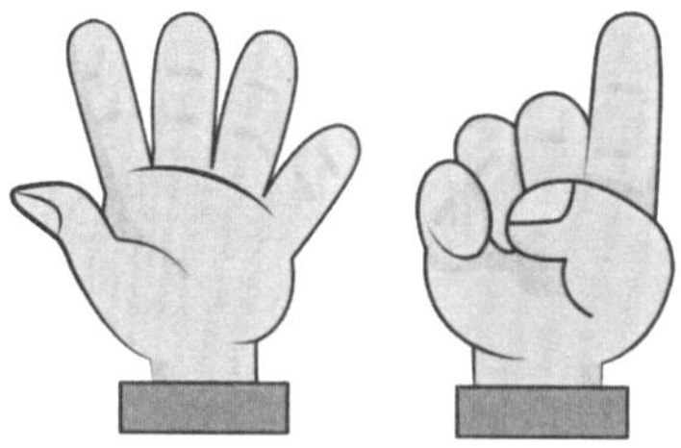

6	7	8

0	1	2

Counting with Fingers: 0-10

How many fingers are there? Circle the correct number.

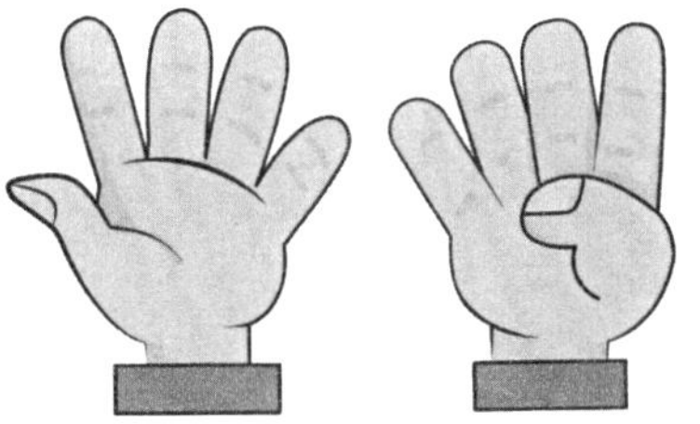

8	9	10

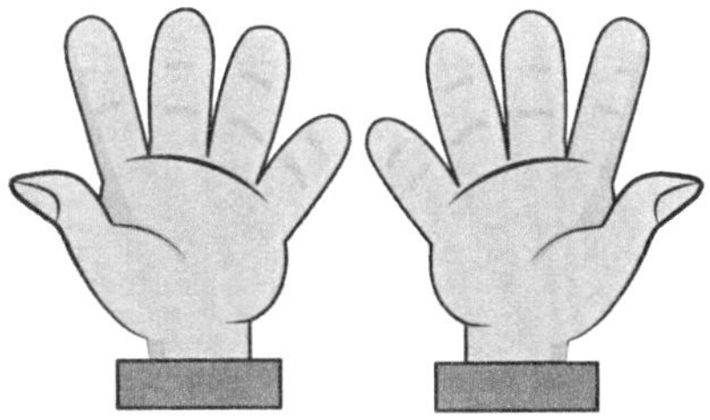

8	9	10

5	6	7

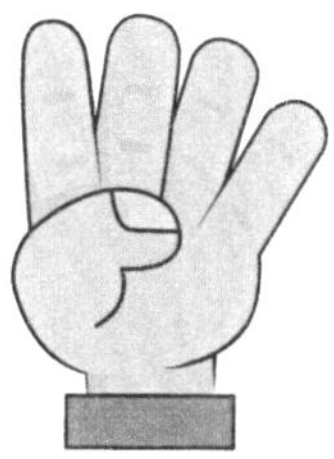

3	4	5

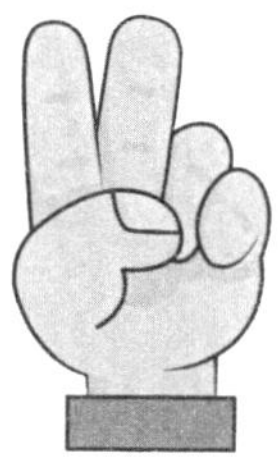

0	1	2

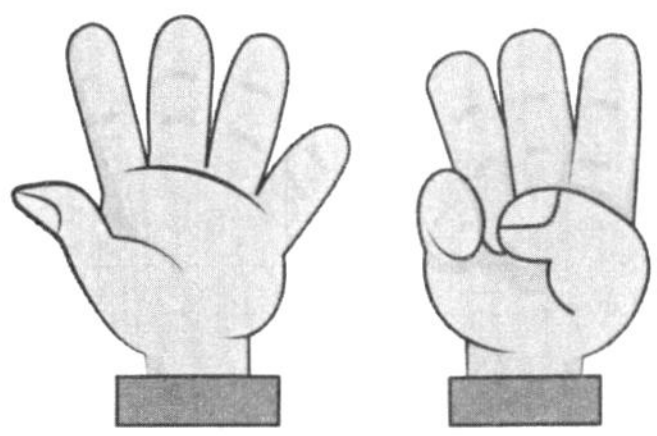

7	8	9

Ten Frames: Match Up

Draw a line from the number to the correct ten frame.

1

5

10

7

4

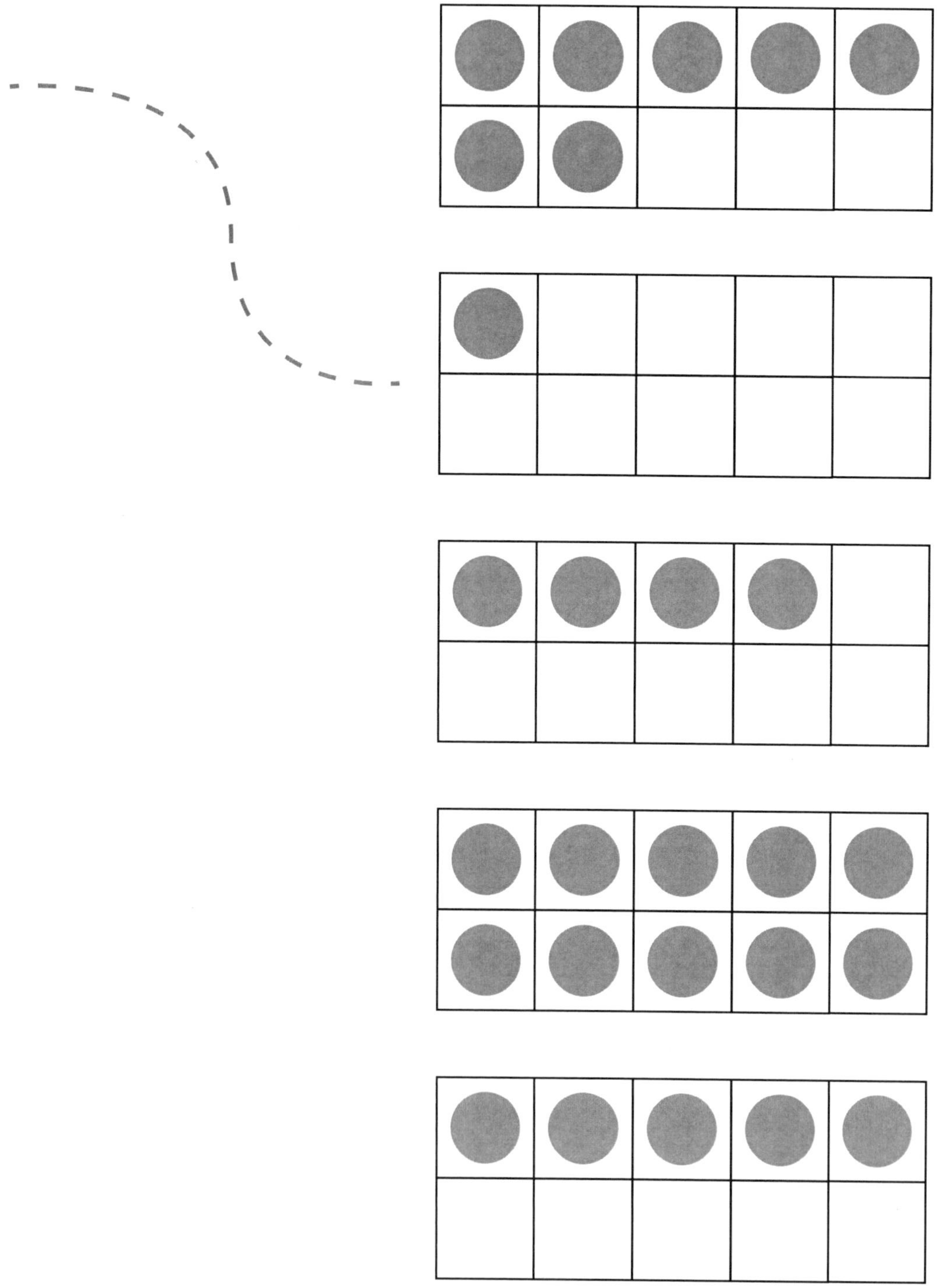

Ten Frames: Match Up

Draw a line from the number to the correct ten frame.

2

8

6

9

3

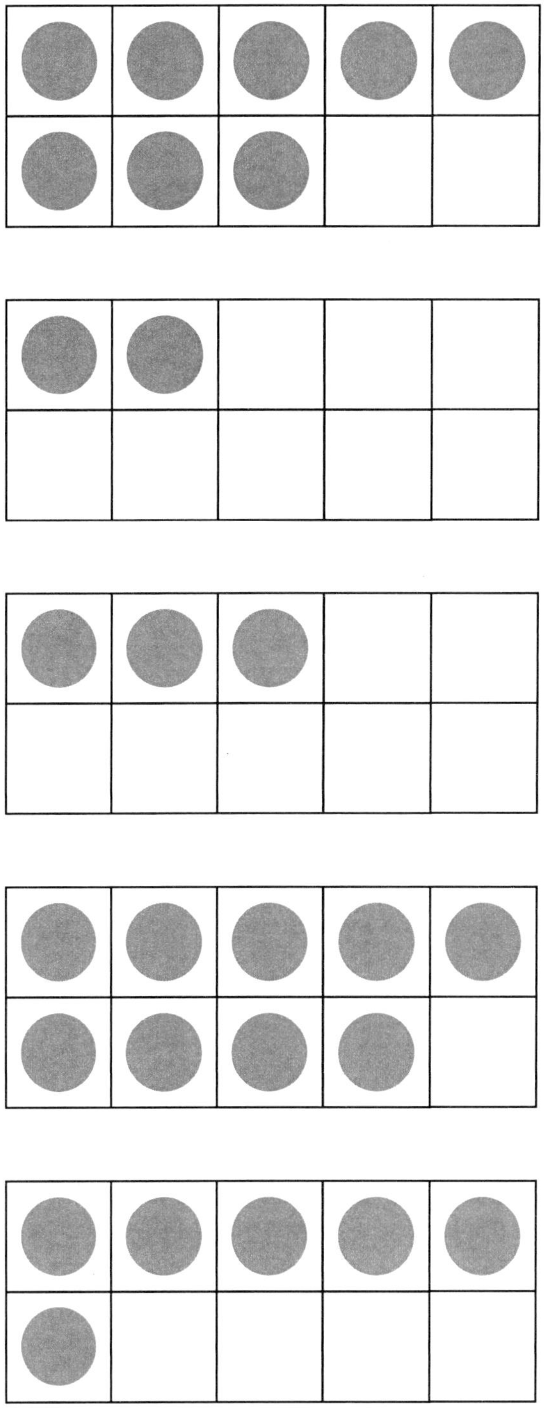

Sums to 5

Use the blocks to add.

2 + 1 = **3**

2 + 2 = ______

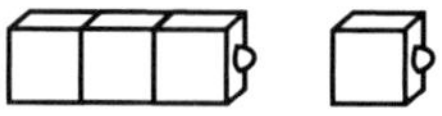

3 + 1 = ______

2 + 3 = ______

3 + 2 = ______

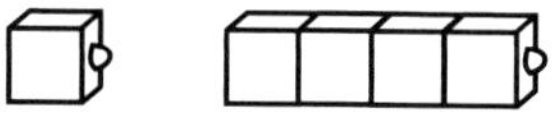

1 + 4 = ______

1 + 1 = ______

1 + 3 = ______

1 + 2 = ______

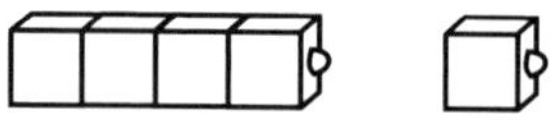

4 + 1 = ______

Sums to 5

Draw ●s to help you add.

● ●●●

1 + 3 = **4**

3 + 2 = ______

2 + 1 = ______

1 + 4 = ______

1 + 2 = ______

3 + 1 = ______

2 + 2 = ______

4 + 1 = ______

2 + 3 = ______

1 + 1 = ______

Colouring by Number: Sums to 5

Colour the object using the colour key.

Think About It!

What happens when you wear a watch on a plane?
Time flies!

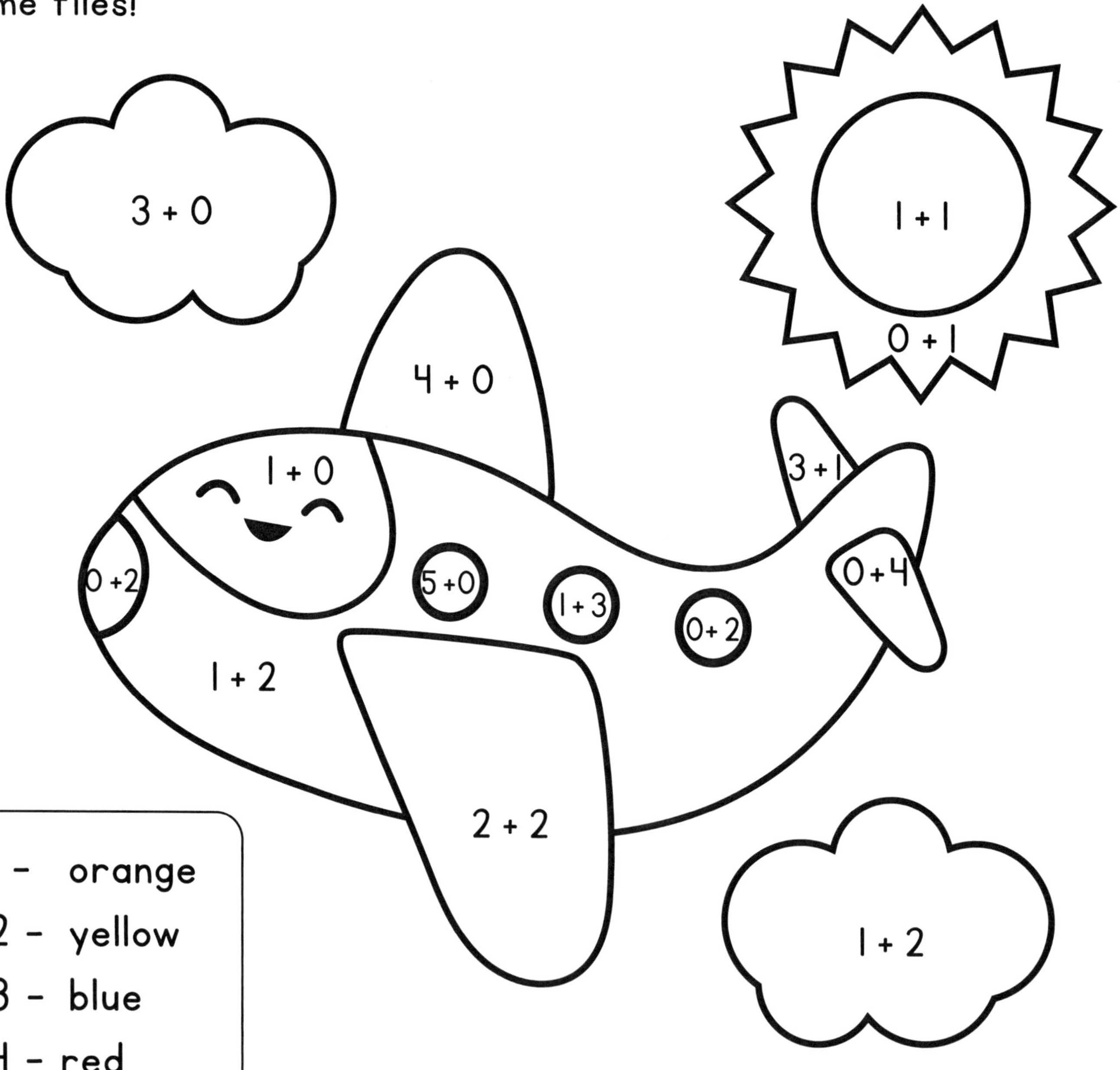

1 - orange
2 - yellow
3 - blue
4 - red
5 - black

Colouring by Number: Sums to 5

Colour the object using the colour key.

Think About It!

What did the dinosaur use to cut wood?
A dino-saw!

1 - orange
2 - yellow
3 - green
4 - grey
5 - blue

Differences to 5

Count the blocks. Cross them out to help you subtract.

1 – 1 = 0

3 – 2 = ____

3 – 1 = ____

5 – 2 = ____

4 – 3 = ____

5 – 4 = ____

5 – 3 = ____

5 – 1 = ____

4 – 2 = ____

4 – 1 = ____

Differences to 5

Draw ●s, then cross them out to help you subtract.

5 – 4 = 1

1 – 1 = ____

5 – 1 = ____

4 – 3 = ____

3 – 1 = ____

3 – 2 = ____

4 – 1 = ____

5 – 2 = ____

5 – 3 = ____

4 – 2 = ____

Colouring by Number: Differences to 5

Colour the object using the colour key.

Think About It!

How do you get a baby to sleep in outer space?
You rocket!

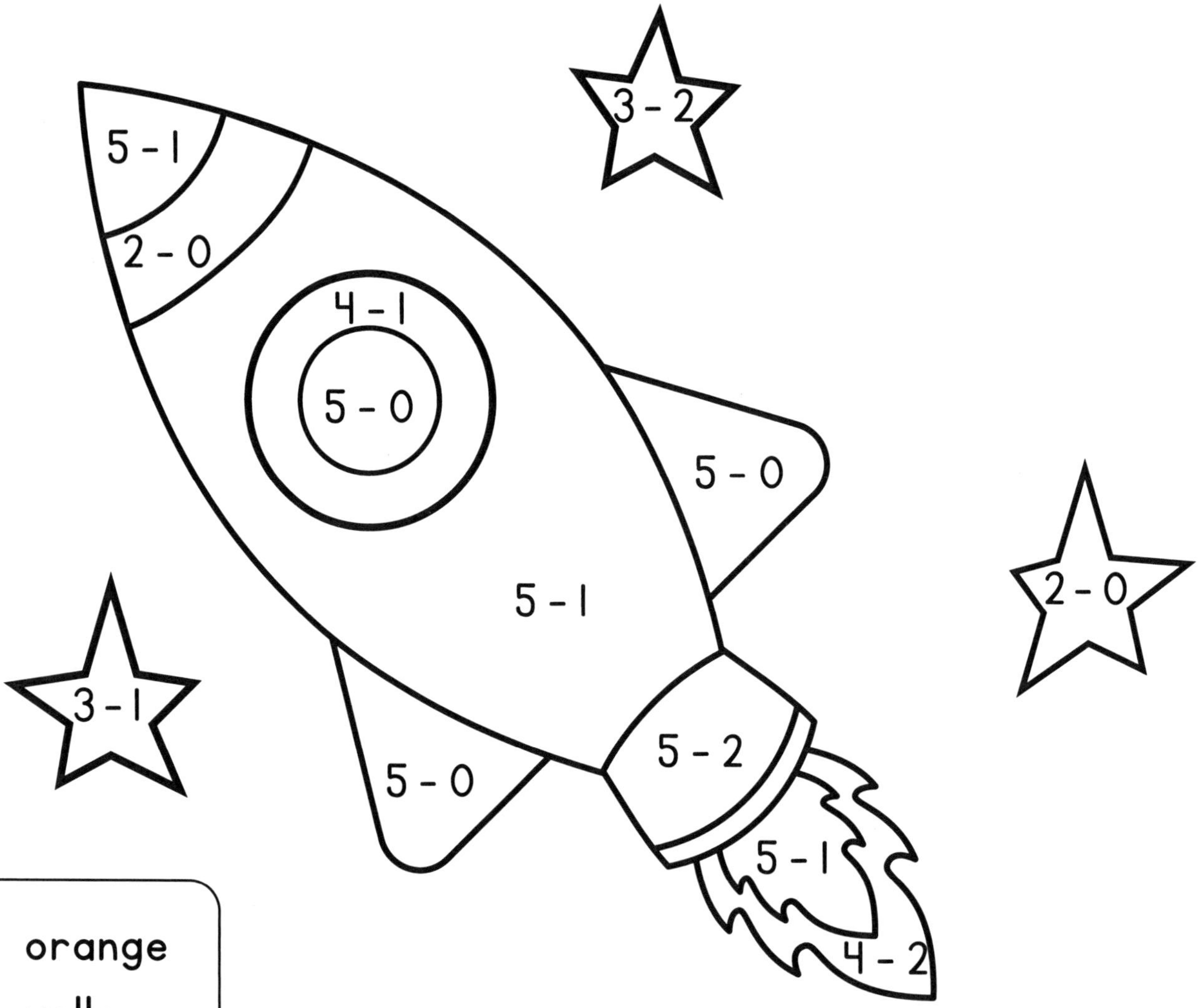

1 - orange
2 - yellow
3 - blue
4 - red
5 - grey

Colouring by Number: Differences to 5

Colour the object using the colour key.

Think About It!

What kind of shoes do mice wear?
Squeakers!

1 - red
2 - yellow
3 - grey
4 - pink
5 - brown

First to Fifth

Circle and colour the first and third butterflies blue.

First Second Third Fourth Fifth

Circle and colour the third and fourth ladybug red.

Circle and colour the second and fifth fish green.

First to Fifth

Circle and colour the first and second monkeys orange.

Circle and colour the fourth and fifth koalas yellow.

Circle and colour the second and fourth eagles purple.

More or Less

Circle the set that has **more**.

Circle the set that has **more**.

Circle the set that has **less**.

More or Less

Circle the set that has **more**.

Circle the set that has **less**.

Circle the set that has **less**.

Counting Fun

Connect the dots by counting to 30.

Think About It!

How do young fish get to school?
By octobus!

Counting Fun

Connect the dots by counting to 30.

Think About It!

What to polar bears eat for lunch?
Ice berg-ers!

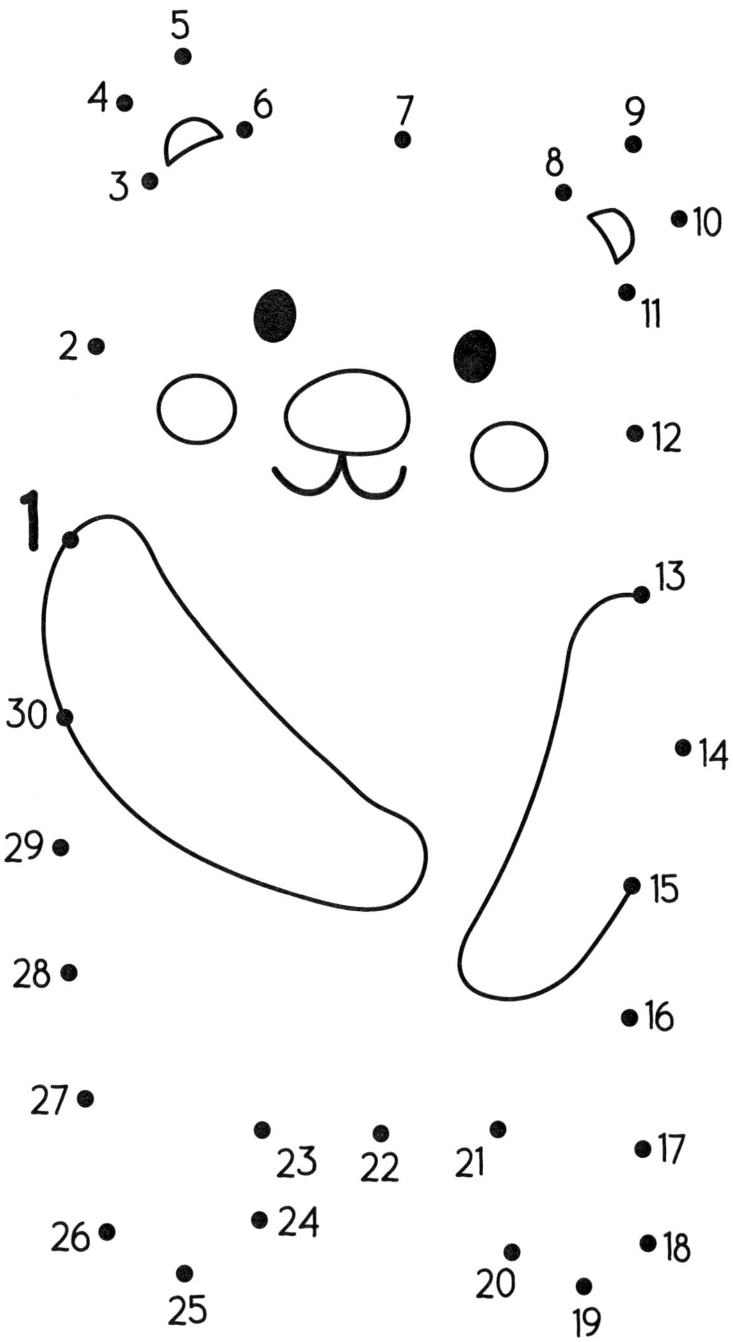

What is Your Phone Number?

Print your phone number.
Use your finger to call your phone number.

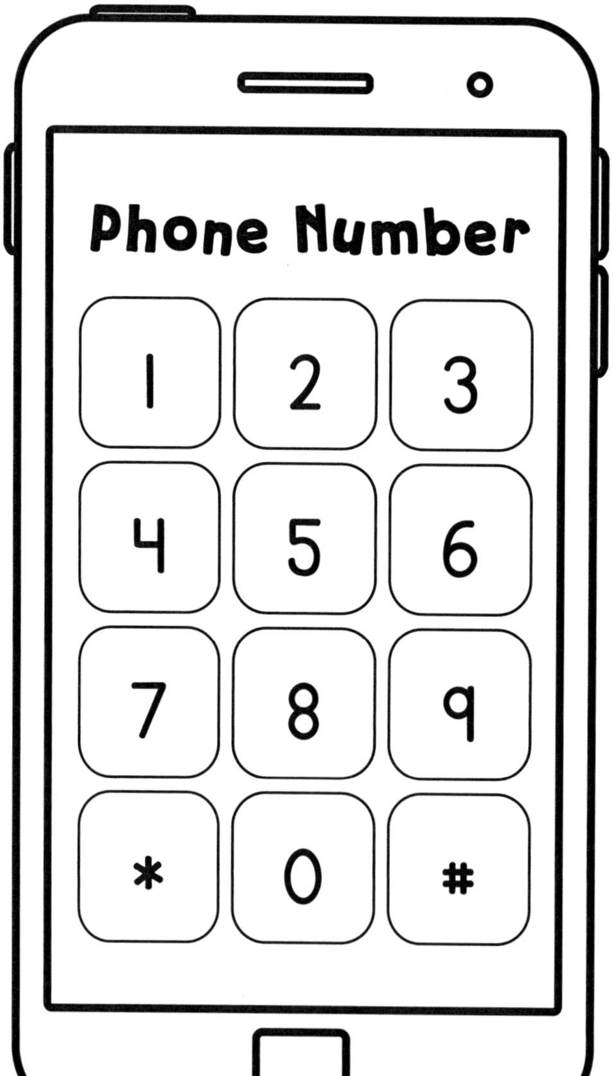

Shapes, Patterns, and Sizes

Get to Know Circles

A **circle** is a shape that is round. Trace the circles.
Colour the circles 

.

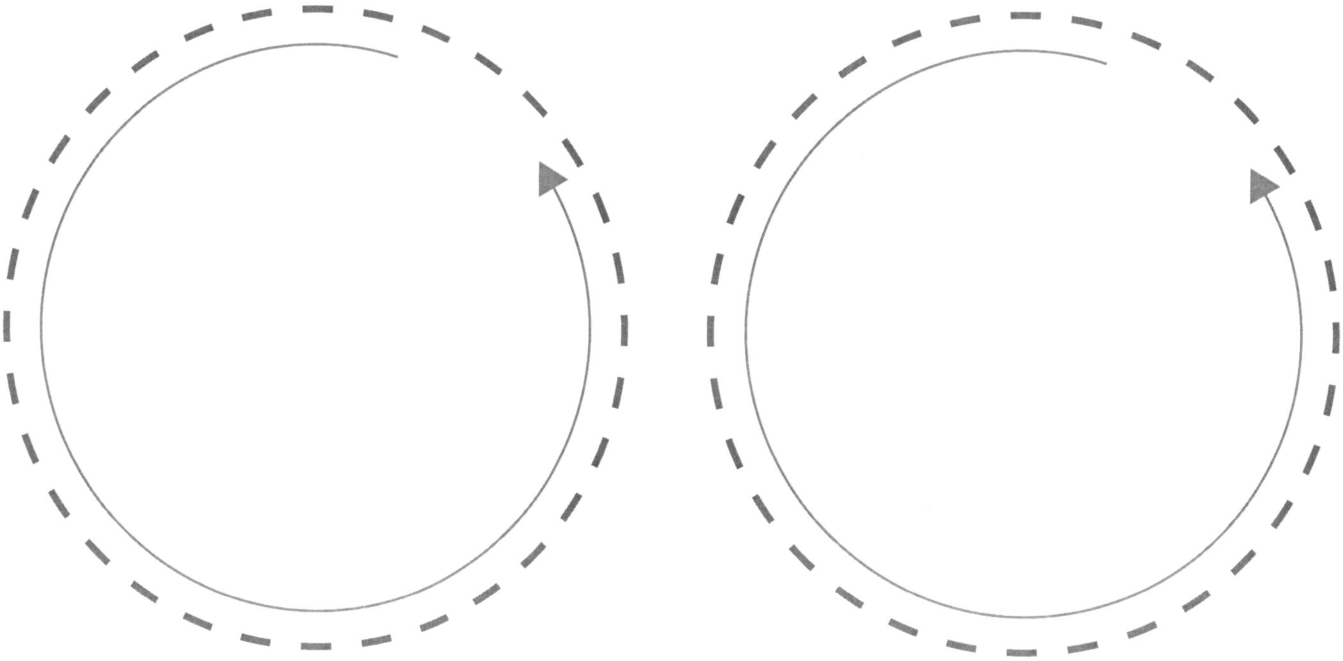

circle

Think About It!

You can find examples of circles all around you!

clock

wheel

Get to Know Squares

A **square** is a shape with four equal sides. Trace the squares.
Colour the squares blue.

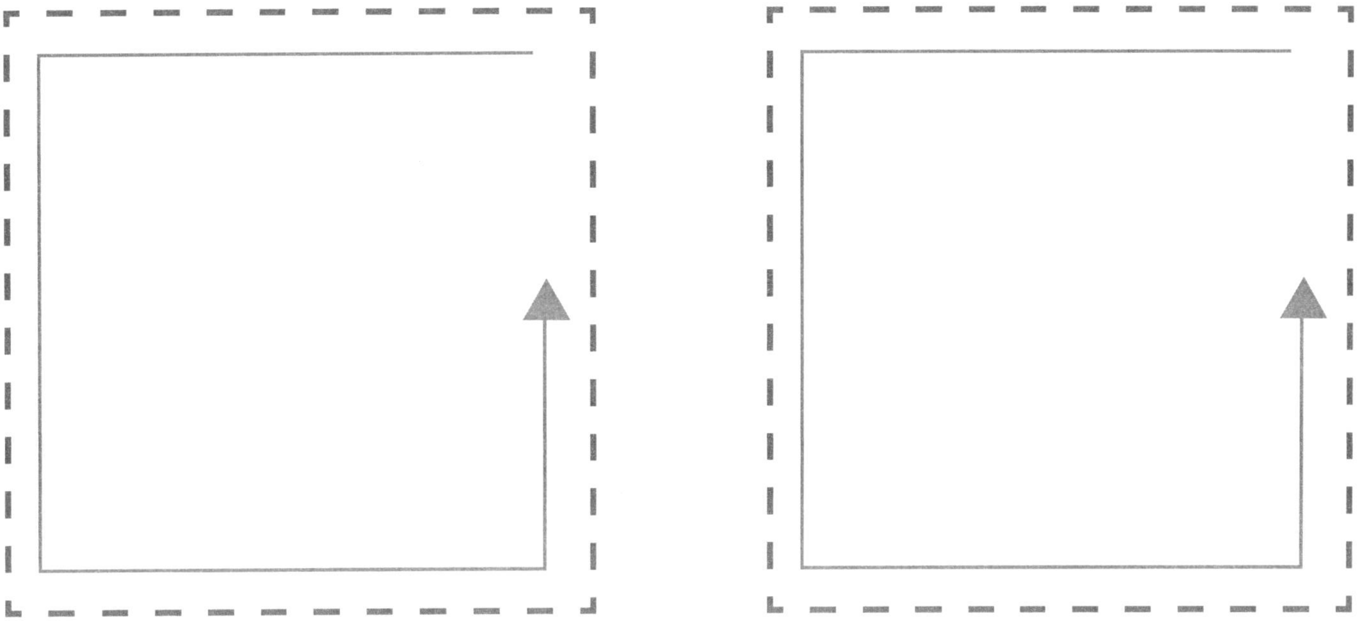

square

Think About It!

You can find examples of squares all around you!

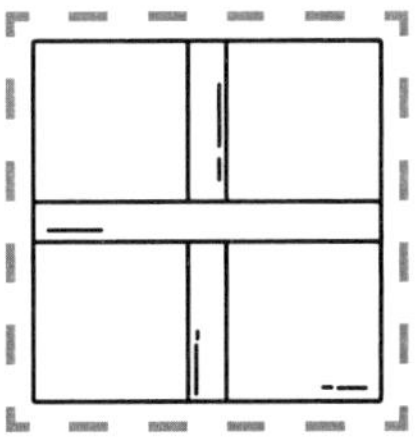

box

blocks

Get to Know Triangles

A **triangle** is a shape with three sides. Trace the triangles.
Colour the triangles **green**.

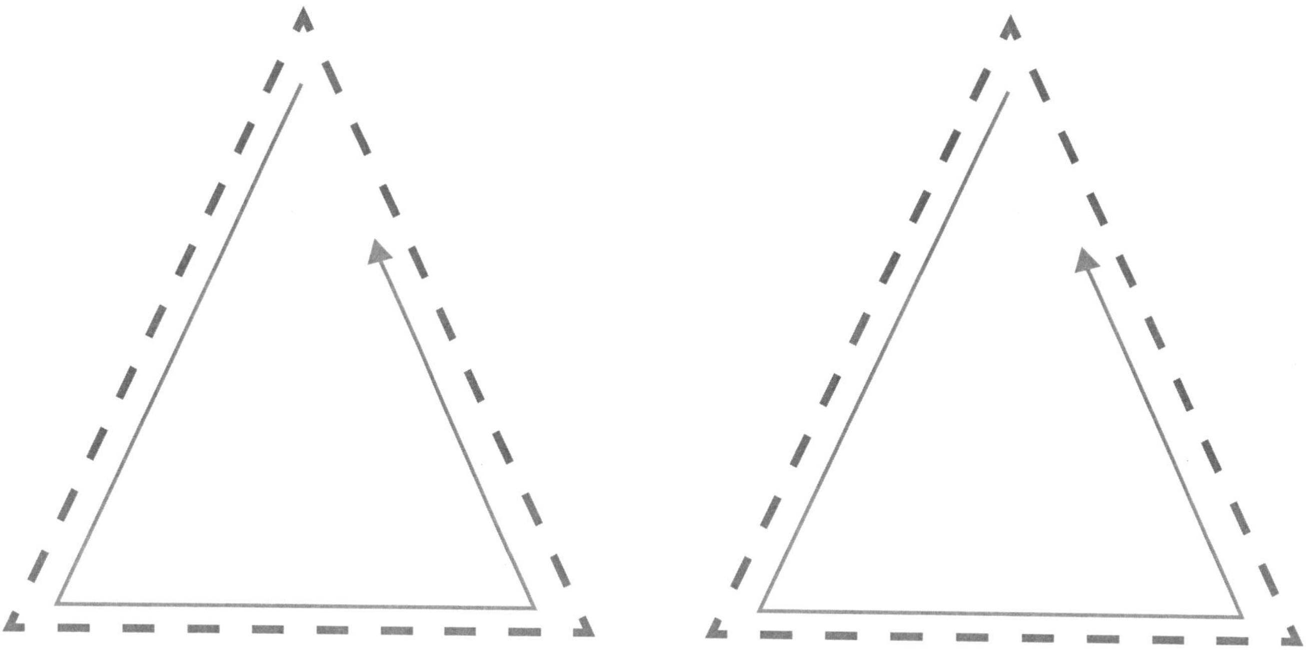

triangle

Think About It!

You can find examples of triangles all around you!

pizza

ice cream cone

Get to Know Rectangles

A **rectangle** is a shape with four sides. Trace the rectangles.
Colour the rectangles **orange**.

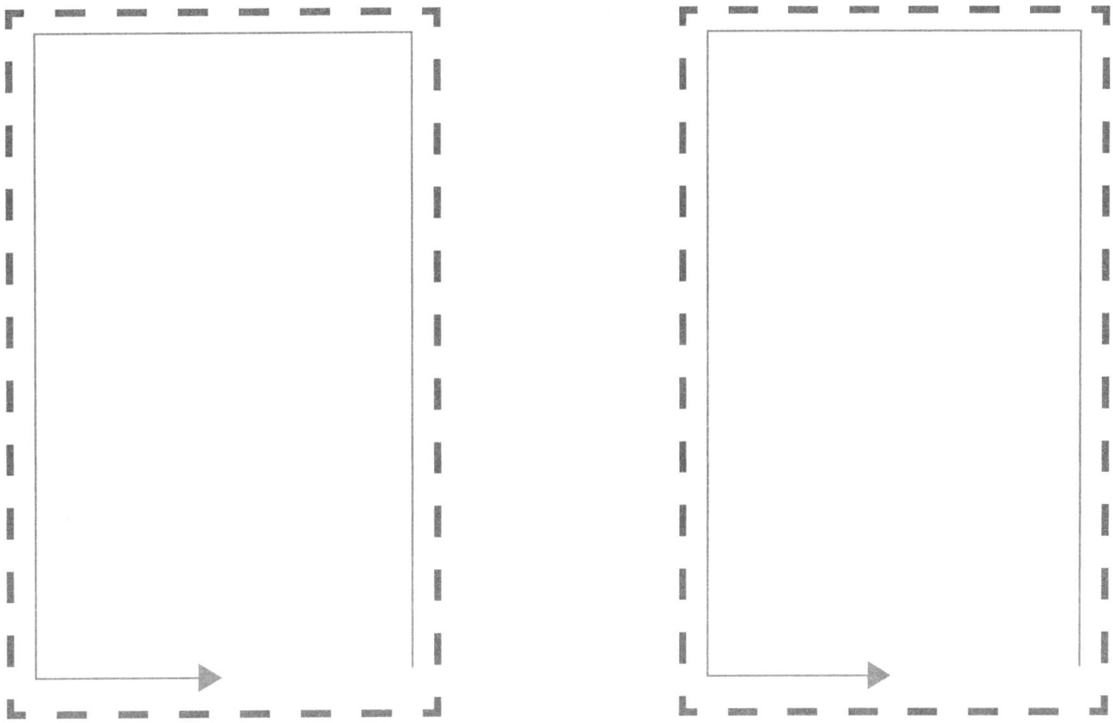

rectangle

Think About It!

You can find examples of rectangles all around you!

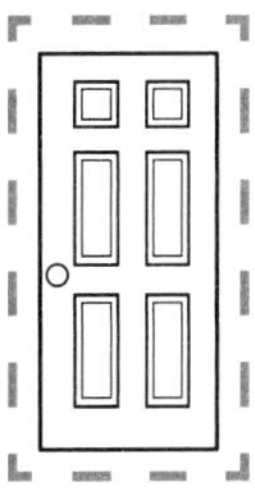

door

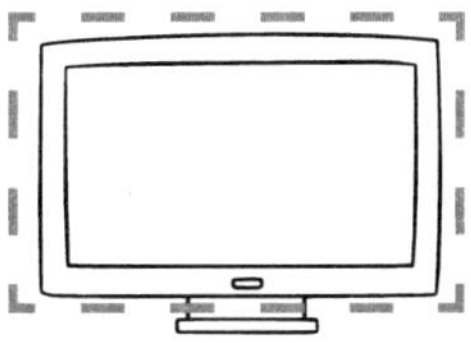

television

Get to Know Ovals

An **oval** is a shape. It is round, but a bit longer in one direction. Trace the ovals. Colour the ovals purple.

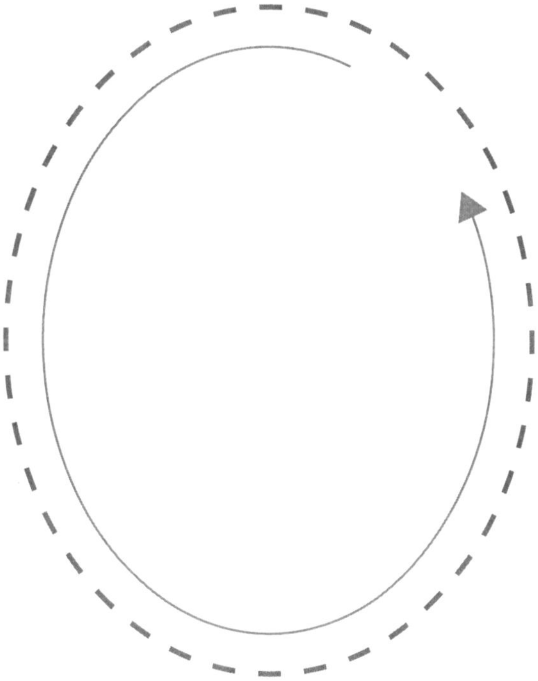

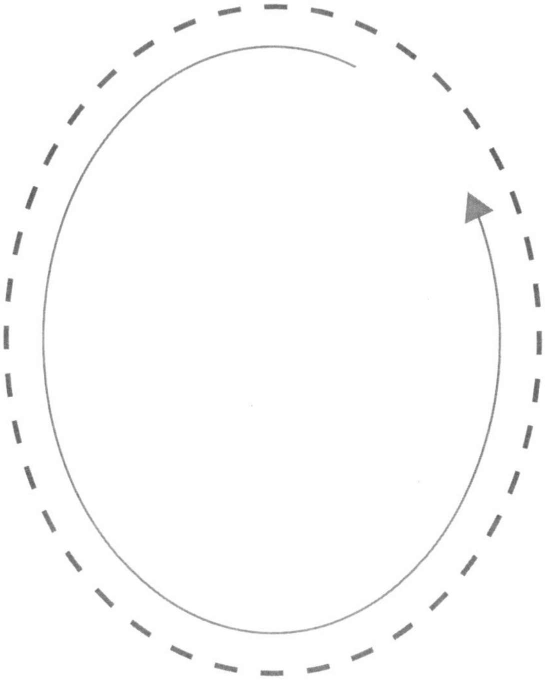

oval

Think About It!

You can find examples of ovals all around you!

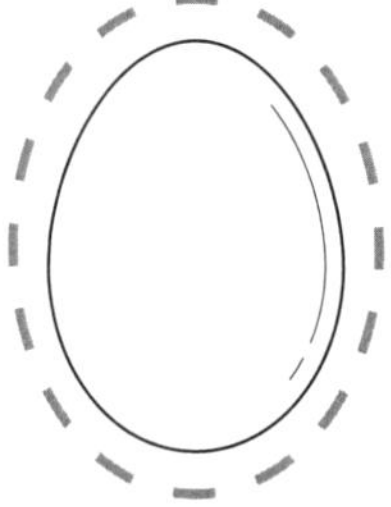

egg

light bulb

Get to Know Diamonds

A **diamond** is a shape with four sides. Trace the diamonds.
Colour the diamonds yellow.

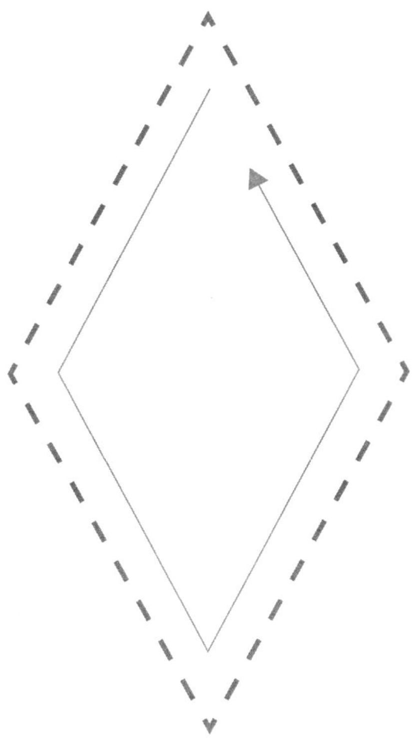

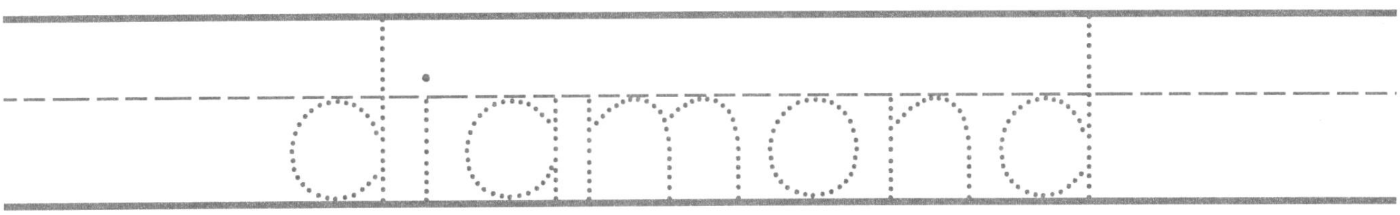

Think About It!

You can find examples of diamonds all around you!

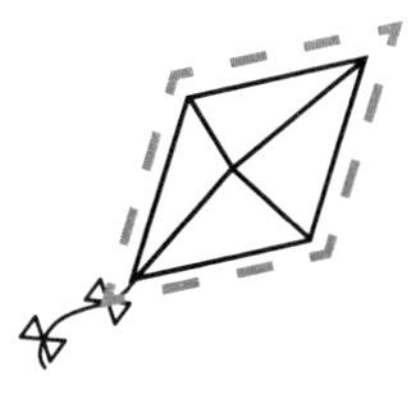

kite

road signs

Shape Colouring Fun

Colour the object using the colouring key.

Colour the circles.	green	Colour the triangles.	red
Colour the squares.	orange	Colour the ovals.	purple
Colour the rectangles.	blue	Colour the diamonds.	yellow

Counting Shapes

Look at the object and count the shapes. Write the number.

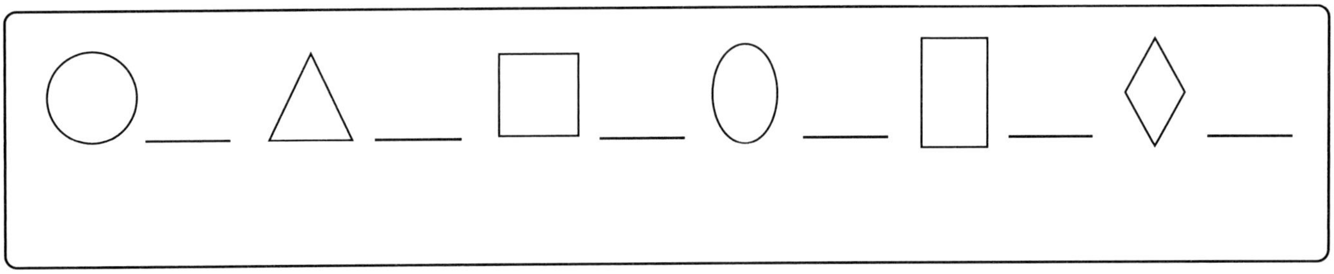

Colour the circles.	red	Colour the triangles.	orange
Colour the squares.	blue	Colour the ovals.	purple
Colour the rectangles.	green	Colour the diamonds.	yellow

Patterning Fun

Look at the pattern.
Colour the next shape in the pattern.

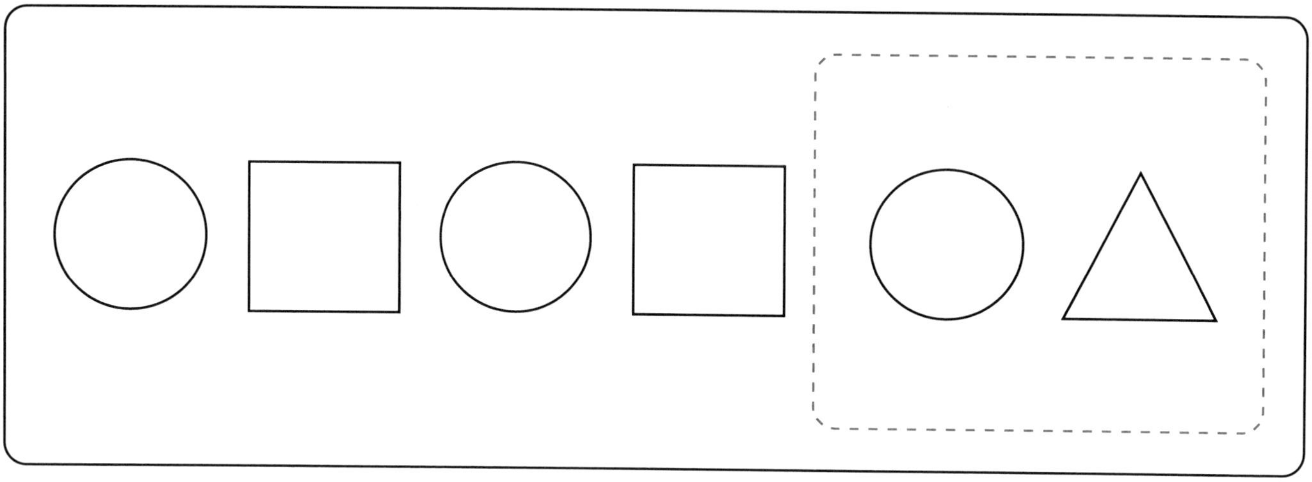

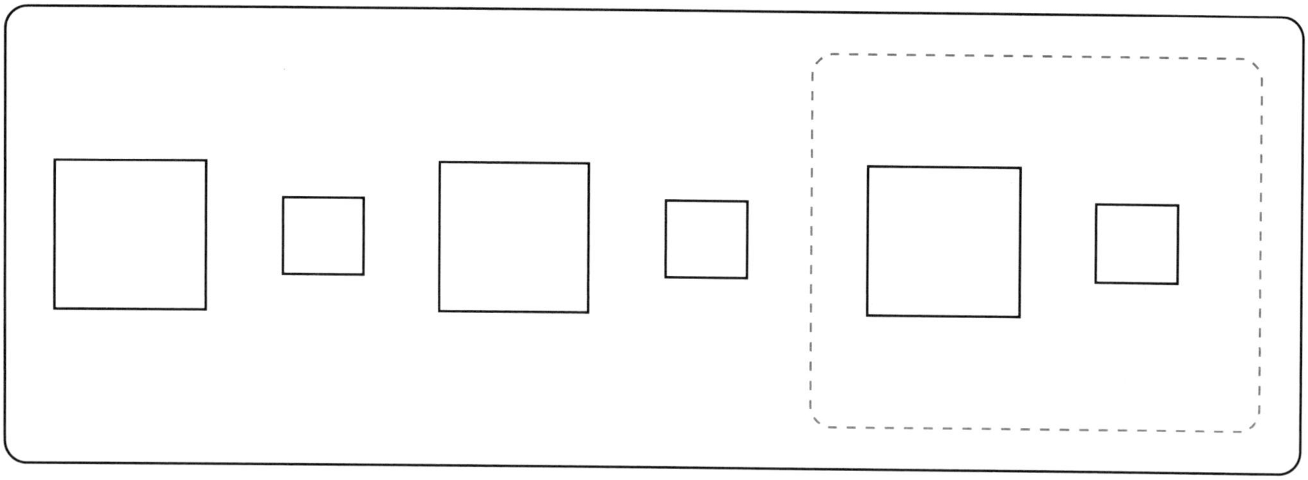

Patterning Fun

Colour in the shapes to make your own colour pattern.

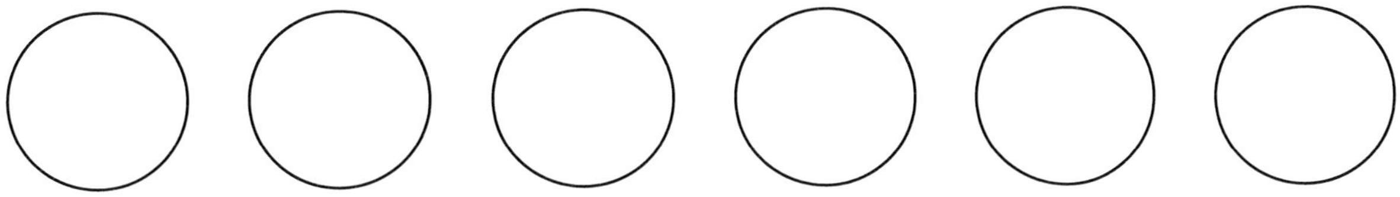

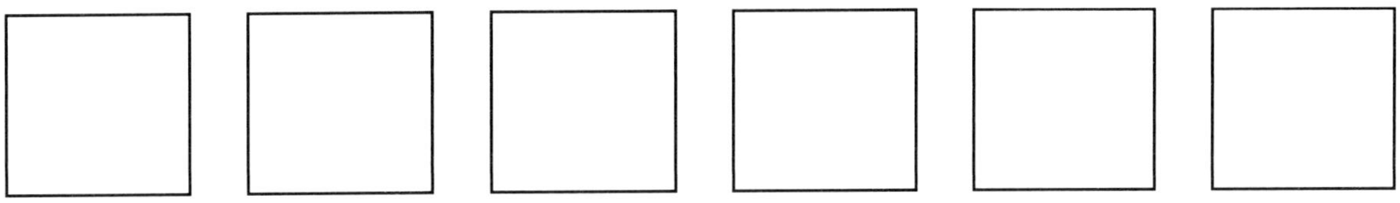

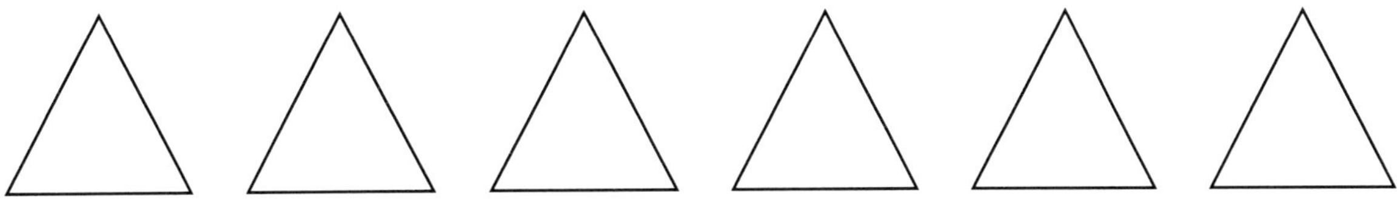

Patterning Fun

Draw what shape comes next in the pattern.
Colour in the shapes to create your own colour pattern.

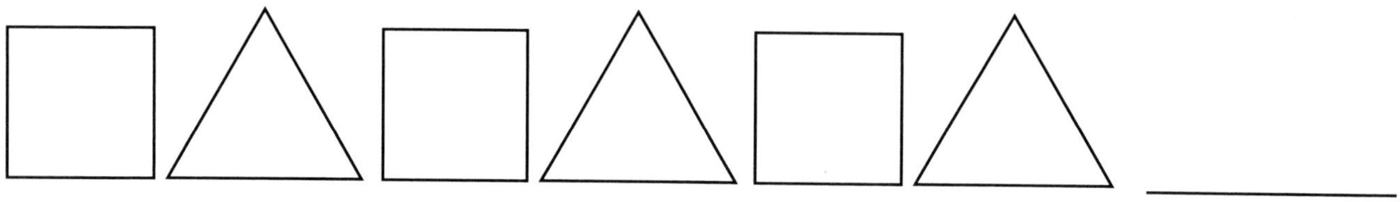

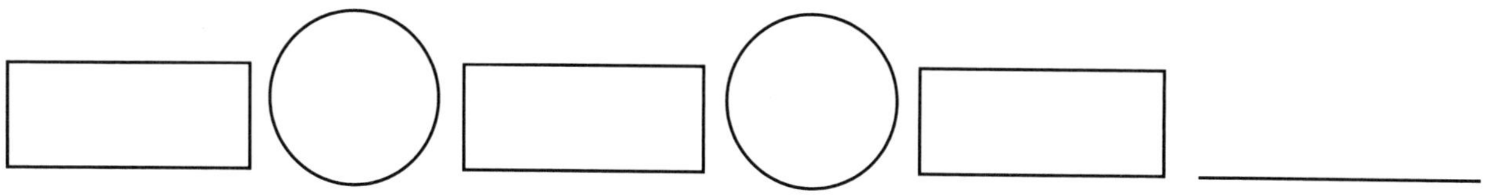

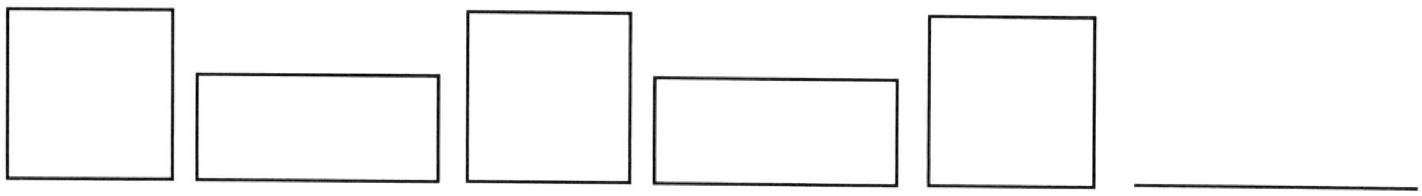

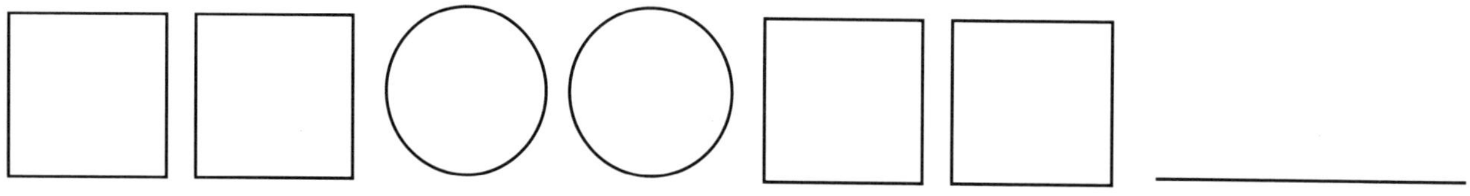

Patterning Fun

Colour in the ice cream scoops to make your own pattern.

Big and Small

Circle the **biggest** goat.

Circle the **smallest** wolf.

Circle the **biggest** horse.

Big and Small

Circle the **smallest** pear.

Circle the **biggest** backpack.

Circle the **smallest** lamp.

Tall and Short

Circle the **tallest** building.

Circle the **shortest** giraffe.

Tall and Short

Circle the **tallest** dessert.

Circle the **shortest** object.

Long and Short

Circle the **longest** key.

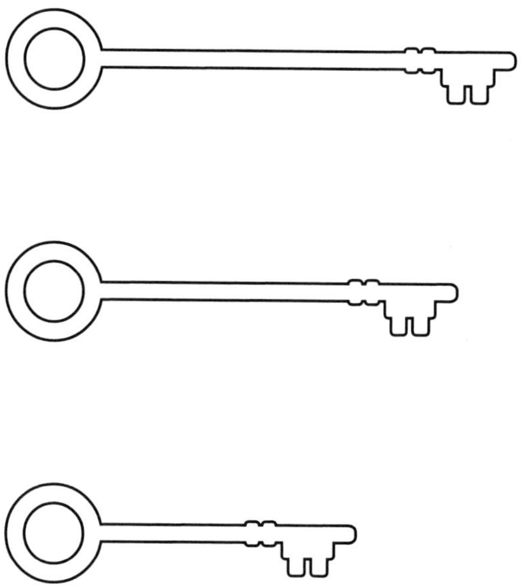

Circle the **shortest** bone.

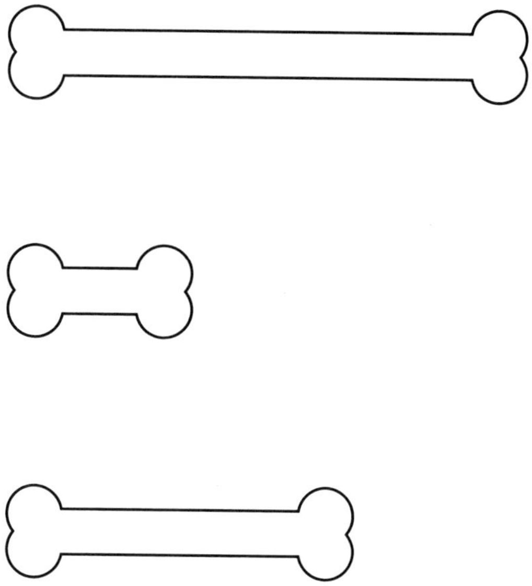

Trace the **longer** rectangle.

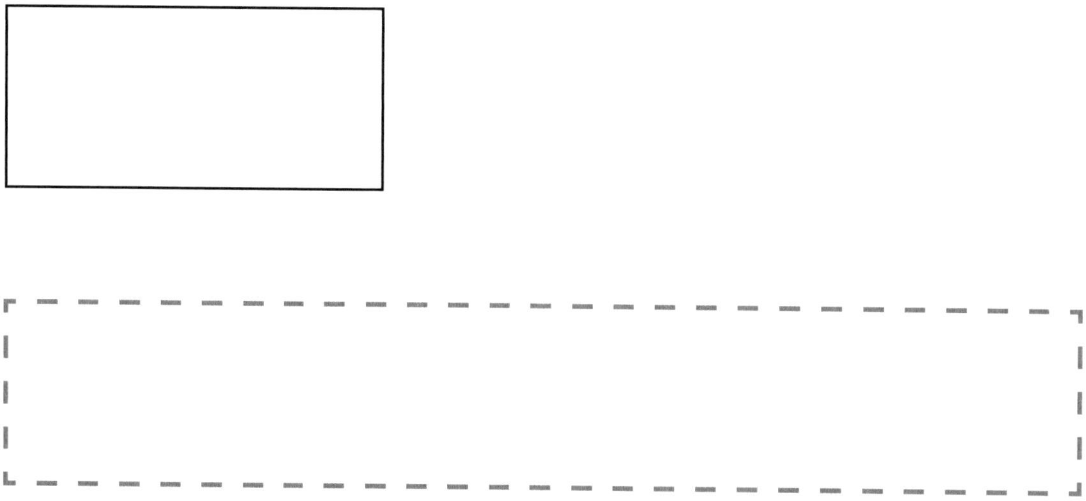

More Learning Skills

Inside and Outside

Read the question in the box and circle the correct answer.

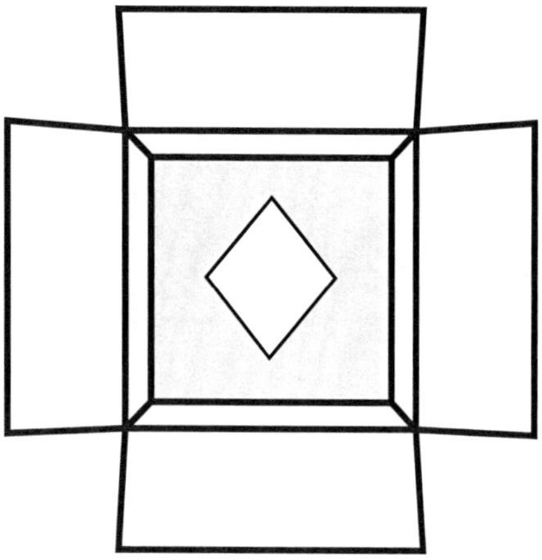

Is the diamond inside or outside the box?

inside outside

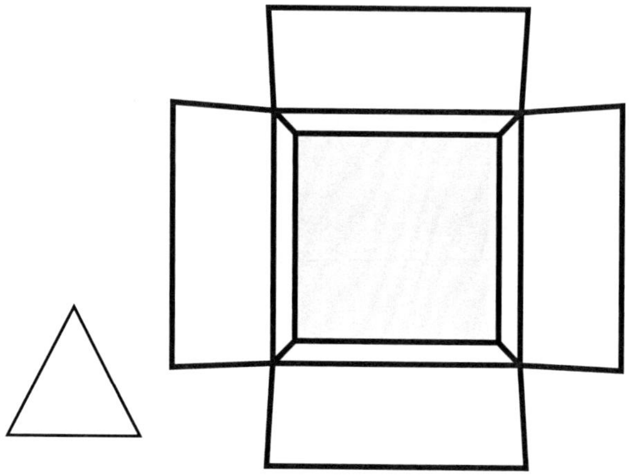

Is the triangle inside or outside the box?

inside outside

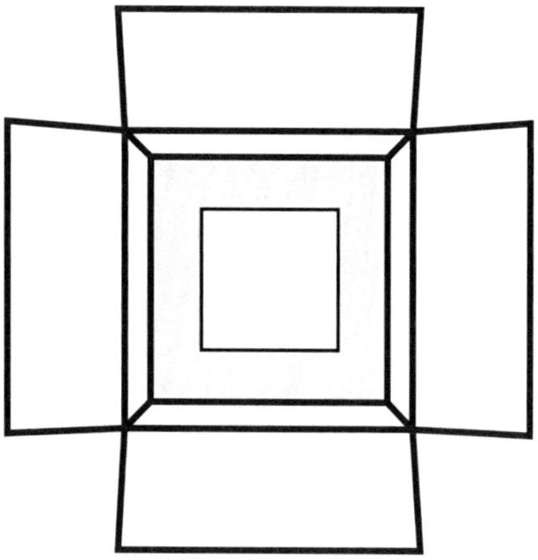

Is the square inside or outside the box?

inside outside

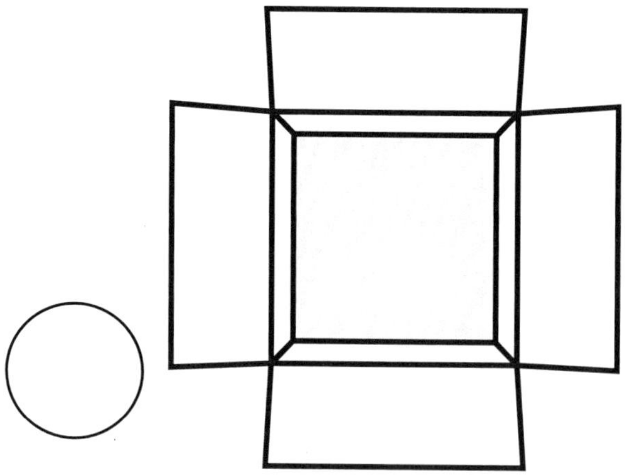

Is the circle inside or outside the box?

inside outside

Inside and Outside

Pack the suitcase! Draw something you need inside the suitcase. Draw something you don't need outside the suitcase.

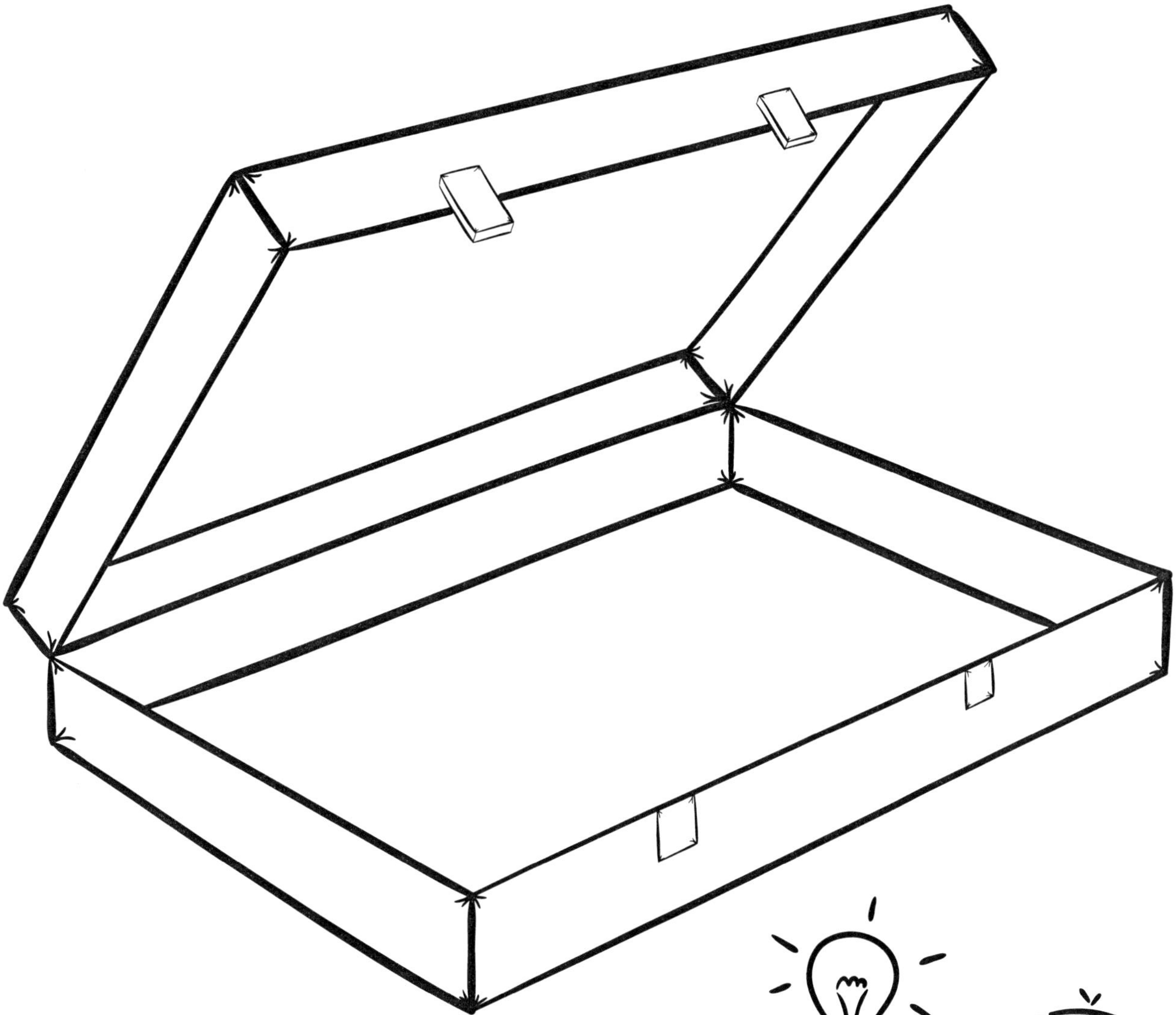

Positional Words

Draw a line from the hamster to the correct positional word.

inside

between

in front of

behind

Positional Words

Draw a line from the dog to the correct positional word.

near

beside

under

on

Get to Know Left and Right

Trace the lines from the left hand to the right hand.
Colour in the objects.

left

right

left

right

left

right

left

right

Get to Know Left and Right

Trace the lines from the right animal to the left animal.
Colour in the animals.

left — right

left **right**

left — right

left **right**

left — right

left **right**

left — right

left **right**

Practice Printing your Name

Print your name on the line below.
Colour in "My Name Is..." in your favourite colour.

My Name Is...

Circle the number of letters in your name.

1	2	3	4
5	6	7	8
9	10	more than 10	

Rhymes, Chants, and Finger Plays

Five Little Speckled Frogs

Five little speckled frogs, *(hold up five fingers)*
Sitting on a speckled log, *(sit down)*
Eating the most delicious bugs...yum, yum. *(pretend to eat)*
One jumped into the pool *(jump)*
Where it was nice and cool.
Then there were four speckled frogs.

Continue until only one frog is left.

One little speckled frog.
Sitting on a speckled log,
Eating the most delicious bugs...yum, yum.
He jumped into the pool
Where it was nice and cool.
Now there are no speckled frogs.

Hickory Dickory Dock

Hickory dickory dock,
The mouse ran up the clock.
The clock struck one,
The mouse ran down.
Hickory dickory dock.

Count to 100 Chant

Hooray! Hooray!
Count to 100 in different ways!

Count by 1s - its really fun!
1, 2, 3, 4, 5...

Count by 2s - I will count with you!
2, 4, 6, 8, 10...

Count by 5s - its easy if you try!
5, 10, 15, 20, 25...

Count by 10s, then start over again!
10, 20, 30, 40...

Rhymes, Chants, and Finger Plays

Ten Fingers

I have ten fingers	*(hold up both hands showing all ten fingers)*
And they all belong to me,	*(point to self)*
I can make them do things.	*(wiggle fingers)*
Would you like to see?	*(point to eyes)*
I can shut them up tight	*(make fists)*
I can open them wide	*(open hands and spread out fingers)*
I can put them together	*(clasp hands together)*
I can make them all hide	*(put hands behind back)*
I can make them jump high	*(hold hands over head)*
I can make them jump low	*(touch the floor with all ten fingers)*
I can fold them up quietly	*(fold hands in lap)*
And hold them just so.	

Who Stole the Cookie?

Who stole the cookie from the cookie jar?

_____________ *(child's name)* stole the cookie from the cookie jar.

(named child) Who me?

(other children) Yes you!

(named child) Couldn't be!

(other children) Then who?

Repeat above verse with the name of a new child.

Tip: The ttheer may wish to have a cookie jar filled with children's name cards. Have a child pick a name card from the cookie jar to start the rhyme.

I'm a Little Teapot

I'm a little teapot,	*(place one hand on hip to imitate a handle)*
Short and stout	*(position other hand in the air to imitate a spout)*
Here is my handle,	
Here is my spout.	
When I get all steamed up	
Hear me shout!	
Tip me over	*(lean to the right to imitate pouring tea from the spout)*
And pour me out!	

Rhymes, Chants, and Finger Plays

It's Raining, It's Pouring

It's raining; it's pouring.
The old man is snoring.
He bumped his head on the top of the bed,
And couldn't get up in the morning.

Twinkle Twinkle Little Star

Twinkle, twinkle, little star,
How I wonder what you are.
Up above the world so high,
Like a diamond in the sky.

Itsy Bitsy Spider

The itsy bitsy spider crawled up the water spout.
Down came the rain, and washed the spider out.
Out came the sun, and dried up all the rain,
and the itsy bitsy spider went up the spout again

Baa, Baa, Black Sheep

Baa, baa, black sheep,
Have you any wool?
Yes sir, yes sir,
Three bags full.
One for the master,
One for the dame,
And one for the little boy
Who lives down the lane

Congratulations!

Great Work!